THE ROAD TO

Mystery of Sanctification: Book II

by

Shan Lu

PUBLISHED BY
KRATOS PUBLISHER

THE ROAD TO FULFILMENT
Copyright ©2022 by Shan Lu
Published by: Kratos Publisher

All rights reserved under international copyright law. No part of this book may be reproduced without permission in writing from the copyright owner, except by a reviewer, who may quote brief passages in a review.

"*Scripture quotations are from The ESV® Bible (The Holy Bible, English Standard Version®), copyright© 2001 by Crossway, a publishing ministry of Good News Publishers, Used by permission. All rights reserved.*"

NASB

"Scripture is taken from the NEW AMERICAN STANDARD BIBLE®, Copyright © 1960,1962,1963,1968,1971,1972,1973,1975,1977,1995 by The Lockman Foundation. Used by permission."

NKJV

Scripture is taken from the New King James Version®. Copyright © 1982 by Thomas Nelson. Used by permission. All rights reserved.

ISBN: 9798368388892

Knowing Shan is what makes me want to read this book. More than our words it's our actions which are "read and seen by all men". Shan is one of the most dedicated "laid down lovers" that I have ever seen. I have watched her passionately seek God out both publicly and privately. She has consistently followed him when few others would. Through dry barren years when she was seemingly all alone, with no one else close by to really encourage her. There are no shortcuts when it comes to intimacy and God is no respecter of persons. He welcomes us all into His heart of hearts; but how many are really willing to seek Him out, obey what He says and make Him their home?

That is what truly sets people apart.

It's easy to feel like a Barnabas when hanging out with Shan. She has grown in leaps and bounds because of pure devotion to Him.

Shan challenges and inspires me without even knowing it. That is certainly a big reason why I would recommend this book.

Pastor Jane McCormack
A Glimpse of Eternity Ministry

"Shan Lu is a dear friend, and a great blessing to the Body of Christ. Her deep devotion to love and serve God with her whole life has a rare quality to it. Marked by a depth of intimacy, integrity and sensitivity to his leading, Shan is dedicated to loving God with all her heart, listening to his voice and following wherever he leads, whatever the cost to her personally. She has particular insight into the process of sanctification and healing that God desires for every one of his children, both as individuals, but also as families and even as nations. In this book, The Road to Fulfilment, Shan explores what it means to grow in spiritual maturity, by overcoming the orphan spirit, which we all have to some degree. She shares vulnerably from her own lived experience and testimony, inviting us all towards greater wholeness and intimacy with our loving Heavenly Father. Shan shows us how much God longs to 're-parent' us, and lovingly deal with the particular wounds we carry from our relationships with our earthly parents, and also our cultures. Her writing is full of Biblical truth, prophetic insight and inspiration, showing us how we can become more Christ-like, and experience the freedom and fulfilment God has for us, as we live out the specific purpose for which we were sent into the world."

Pastor Sophie Earl
His House

Dedication

To my Lord Jesus, the lover of my soul, for whom I was created and exist, to whom I cling through all seasons of my walk, and with whom I am one unto eternity.

To my Dada God, my eternal home, from whom I came, to whom I belong, and in whose arms I am a little child, finding complete love, acceptance, and rest.

To my faithful Friend, the Holy Spirit, with whom I share the passion for glorifying the Son and who teaches, guides, comforts, and strengthens me in this journey.

Acknowledgements

I would like to express a special gratitude to my dear friends Ian and Jane McCormack, who have discipled me and played an instrumental part in my spiritual growth over the years, particularly concerning developing personal intimacy with God. Being such precious gifts and blessings to the body yet so humble and unassuming, they lead by example and have often served me like a father and mother would a child, both in the spiritual and the natural. Ian and Jane, may the Lord bless and reward you for all you have poured into my life!

I thank the Lord for entrusting me with this assignment, which has been the most enormous undertaking in my life, and for granting me the grace to complete it, without which it would have been impossible. The process of writing in and of itself has been a journey of growth for me. I pray that the Lord will accomplish everything He wants to do through this book (and the other books of the *Mystery of Sanctification* series) and that He will receive all the glory.

Contents

Dedication	4
Acknowledgements	5
I. Introduction	10
II. Grow In Sonship	22
i. Exile and Homecoming	22
ii. The Parable of The Prodigal Son	33
iii. A Personal Testimony	42
iv. An Exhortation from The Author	61
III. The Sanctification in The Family	64
i. The Redemption of Family	64
ii. The Spiritual Umbilical Cord	73
iii. Overcoming in The Family	83
iv. From Brokenness to Wholeness	116
v. The Masculine and Feminine Traits of God	124
vi. The Corporate Significance	143
vii. A Final Note	147
IV. The Treasures of All Nations	150

I.

Introduction

I am very excited that I get to write about the Father in this book. The sheer thought of Him, His goodness, and His all-encompassing love toward me; overwhelms me.

Sitting on the floor of my little rented room that looks somewhat dark at this time, I can feel His heart towards me and the wave upon wave of His love flowing from His throne where He is seated, flooding my being.

Ah, He too, is excited that I am writing about Him!

What a joy to share His heart with His other children! And what a hope to bring many more little ones closer to Him and see them find

Introduction

breakthrough, freedom, and rest in Him! Only that, how would my writing ever do You justice, my dear Papa?

It is such a wonderful feeling being cocooned in the Father's love, deeply assured of His acceptance, and at peace with myself, as one created by Him to walk with Him, a beloved daughter who joyfully looks forward to all the good plans her Father has for her.

I think 'fulfilment' is the word.

Mankind is created in such a way that we feel most fulfilled when we '**live** and **move** and **have our being**' in God[1]. When we 'live' in God, we find the reason for our existence – to be in a relationship with the Creator, or else we may find life in this world meaningless, hopeless, lonely, and depressing, and some might even have suicidal thoughts. When we 'have our being' in God, we find our identity as sons, much loved and cared for by our heavenly Father, or else we would be carrying the orphan heart, struggling with insecurity and anxiety, and exhausted from striving. When we 'move' in God, we find our purpose and calling as individuals and step into the wonderful plans the Father has for our lives, or else we are likely to be enslaved to making a living out of the fear of lack, feeling bound and suffocating.

I know the above may sound a little clichéd to some, but the real question is, why do we often see a mismatch between what seems to be theologically accurate and what we experience in reality? Are all Christians set free from, for example, loneliness, depression, insecurity, anxiety, and the fear of lack? Have all Christians stepped into the callings of their lives and been finding their walks with God exhilarating? Are we supposed to always accept that unspeakable element of disappointment in our Christian faith and secretly resign ourselves to the experience-derived conclusion that the amazing promises of God in the Bible are often more

Introduction

theoretical than actually unattainable? Is God Yes and No? What are we missing here?

The journey.

In my walk, I have discovered that, from obtaining the name 'sons of God' upon being born again to living like 'sons of God' [2], there is a whole **journey of rehabilitation.**' As much as it is exciting to celebrate the homecoming of a prodigal, it would usually take years for him to be able to shed all the orphan habits that he picked up while wandering in the world. As much as it is wonderful to witness the new spiritual birth of a person, it would take years for a baby to grow to mature manhood to comprehend and enjoy his relationship with the Father to the full. Jesus said, *"I came that they may have life and have it ABUNDANTLY"*[3].

What has prevented us from having life 'abundantly' is often our unawareness or neglect of the journey that lies beyond the point of adoption as sons and the part that we ought to play to further our spiritual growth.

Before being reconciled with God through Jesus Christ, we were strangers to the Father's love, acceptance, comfort, and provision. Instead, we learnt from the world how to survive, and having learnt how to survive, we operate out of survival mode even when we are back at the Father's house[4]. Survival mode is a way of being that is of an orphan rather than a son, and that compels us to embark on an endless quest for a sense of security, belonging, purpose, achievement, recognition, etc. We are consumed by it, and yet it never seems enough. Though we have become born-again, we are stuck in such a mode because of our old self, and its riddance is neither automatic nor circumventable. What the Father had in mind when He sent His Son to die for us, however, was that in Christ, not only would we have a right standing before Him, but by our continually and

Introduction

INTENTIONALLY choosing to live according to God's ways in the subsequent 'journey of rehabilitation,' we would also **be healed, restored and conformed to the image of the Son**, living up to the name 'sons of God' on every level, that Jesus might, in a genuine sense, be the firstborn among many brothers [5].

In my journey, the event that enabled me to experience a significant leap in the newness of life as a son was being healed of a series of family wounds. And I have since realised that the state of one's relationship with his earthly father and mother is inseparable from the quality of his relationship with the heavenly Father because we commonly subconsciously use the former as a reference for the latter. The last verse of the last book of the Old Testament, *"turn the hearts of fathers to their children and the hearts of children to their fathers,"* conveys a profound longing of the Father's heart – turning the hearts of the sons of man back to Him, the Father of all [6], and a means

Introduction

where we can get to know the first person of the Trinity and grow in sonship, for real.

The Word says, *"All have sinned and fall short of the glory of God"* [7]. As a consequence of the Fall, as individuals, we all have inherited the sinful nature/lusts of the flesh/sinful tendencies from our earthly fathers and mothers. Our souls have been wounded in different ways and to varying degrees by our parents' yielding to such when bringing us up. It is only by crucifying such sinful nature (and I will explain how in the book) that we can partake more in God's divine nature and receive healing for our souls [8]. Through this, we grow more into the image and stature of Christ [9], who is the image of God [10], WHO IS LOVE [11], and who empowers us to love our fathers and mothers unconditionally with His perfect love, overlooking their faults and weaknesses. The heart change on our part then brings about the reconciliation. Such a spiritual transformation within us also frees our children and our children's children from the

Introduction

generational patterns of sins in the family line. It becomes a spiritual inheritance that we can leave to our posterity. I refer to this process as **'the sanctification in the family.'**

Personally, I have benefited hugely from such in terms of finding WHOLENESS. Even though I am far from being all sorted, I have been able to experience tremendous peace, rest and freedom as a result of it. I believe that sanctification is the will of God for all of us [12], and the sanctification in the family is a part of it.

Admittedly, this process is not the easiest, as it involves revisiting deep childhood wounds. However, unless we allow the Father to take our hands and take us back to where the damage was done and let Him **re-father** and **re-mother** us in those areas (in doing so, help turn our hearts to our fathers and mothers), we would not be able to truly walk in the newness of life as sons finding healing, freedom, love, and acceptance in the Father. This

Introduction

is because God designed human families in such a way that our well-being and spiritual soundness are directly tied to the condition of our hearts toward our fathers and mothers. Besides, it is by intimately journeying and communing with the Father in this reasonably deep part of sanctification, in which we fully open ourselves to Him, all our pains and struggles, and let Him help us untangle them all and redeem the past, that we get to know what the Father is really like.

Furthermore, I have discovered that another beautiful fruit of sanctification in the family is restoring and rebalancing God's masculine and feminine traits in us. God is Spirit [13], He is neither male nor female, yet He has both masculine characteristics, such as defender, passion for justice, reasoning, decision-making, problem-solving, and initiative, and feminine traits, such as empathy, compassion, intuition, and the ability to comfort and nurture. As men and women made in the image of God, we all reflect those

Introduction

characteristics, though falling short of the glory of God means that we no longer bear such to the perfect degree or proportion. However, by being re-fathered and re-mothered by the heavenly Father, we can tap into the original reservoir of God's masculinity and femininity to have our masculine and feminine traits repaired and reinstated to their optimal mix. Therefore, we can become who God has created us to be as men and women. Our collective overcoming of the orphan spirit, including restoring masculine and feminine traits and their balance, helps cultivate a healthy church environment where believers fellowship not out of neediness, nor is there pressure to perform, and where all members of the body are allowed to grow without a ceiling and fulfil their functions as ordained by God.

Finally, in addition to growing in sonship through reconciling with our fathers and mothers in the heart, our reconciliation with our own **national identity** is crucial to becoming who God has called us to be and fulfilling our God-given destinies, both as individuals and as people. Many nations worldwide have historically suffered the injustice of imperialism and colonialism, and their peoples still have to deal with the spiritual aftermath of such today, including my home country China. Through the experience of reconciling with my Chinese identity, I can see that learning to relate in a godly way to those nations that historically wronged us, i.e., neither idolatry nor resentment, matters not only to our own breakthrough and freedom, but also the development of the body as a whole. It allows the churches in the nations to foster their respective Christian heritages with distinct cultural characteristics and bring them as treasures into the house of the Lord to make it beautiful and glorious.

While nations of the world compete in the military and economic might, nations that are the greatest in God's eyes and most esteemed in heaven are the ones that serve other nations most [14]. Like those

Introduction

'sheep nations' in Matthew 25:31-46 (KJV), they will inherit the kingdom of heaven. And this, unlike the temporal interests in this world, is an eternal heritage.

Through the chapters, you will see my personal struggles in the things mentioned above and how I was able to break through, as well as the revelations received along the way. I hope that by sharing them, you will know that you are not alone in this journey, that God's promises are both true and achievable, and that with the guidance and empowerment of the Holy Spirit, you can overcome and find **The Road to Fulfilment.**

1. (Act 17:28) **2.** (Gal 4:4-7; Rom 8:15-16) **3.** (Joh 10:10) **4.** (Eph 2:19) **5.** (Rom 8:29) **6.** (Mal 4:6; Eph 4:6) **7.** (Rom 3:23) **8.** (2Pe 1:3-4) **9.** (Eph 4:22,24; 2Co 3:18; Col 3:9-10; 1Co 15:49) **10.** (Joh 14:9; 2Co 4:4; Col 1:15) **11.** (1Jn 4:8,16) **12.** (1Th 4:3) **13.** (Joh 4:24) **14.** (Mat 20:25-27)

II.

Grow In Sonship

i. Exile and Homecoming

Like many of the younger generations in China, I had a rigorous upbringing. Born in the 80s, growing up, my parents had very high expectations of me. They did their utter best to afford me excellent educational opportunities, including all sorts of private tuition, 'special attention' from teachers (via networking), and, last but not least, overseas studies when studying abroad for Chinese students were not yet common. My parents sacrificed a lot for me, both financially and mentally, in the hope that I would excel and one day stand on my own two feet, becoming successful and prosperous, and never have to experience the kind of hardship their generation went through.

I was obedient to my parents. Wishing to please them, I worked very hard and performed well. I was accepted into the best junior and senior high schools in our region with top marks and competed in maths competitions. I got straight A's at A-levels and went on to read at one of the best universities in the UK, from which I earned a first-class honours degree. I was then employed by a top US investment bank in London and started my career as a trader with an initial salary tripling what most of my peers would have been earning at that time. Afterward, I worked in Human Resource Management at the headquarters of a nationwide Chinese commercial bank in southern China.

Besides, I was never the nerdy type but was always active in extracurricular activities. I started learning the keyboard/piano when I was 6. Throughout my school years, I frequently participated in school performances such as singing, dancing, drama, and poem recitation and was the host of various school events. I was the representative of the art and music classes, the conductor of the school orchestra and national anthem, the vice-president of the student union, and the head of the broadcast station, among other things. I represented my university by competing in the Latin and Ballroom dance competitions in the British student circuit and received numerous medals and trophies. I was also a social secretary for the club.

In the eyes of many, especially among family, friends, and relatives, I was that 'perfect kid', 'an example of excellence'... Most importantly, I made my parents proud.

Yet, what I have not told you is the sense of insecurity that I constantly struggled with, the endless fear and anxiety about how others perceived me and about the future, the many sleepless nights that I suffered due to pressure, the mental exhaustion from striving, the alcohol I downed and the other things I did to fit in despite myself... and worst of all, the ever-present tormenting feeling of emptiness and purposelessness of life. *I have it all, so what? I am stuck here in a life that is all about fulfilling my obligations and others' expectations. Then one day, I die and turn into nothingness. Is that it? How pathetic! I might as well die now, cutting short a few years of meaninglessness. My parents may moan over me for a while, but soon no one will remember me.* At times, I contemplated such...

But thanks be to God! He found me. Having formed and set me apart in my mother's womb, He watched over me all my life [1], and patiently waited for me to call Him **'Abba! Father!'** [2]

I know in this world, there are many like the old me living in survival mode despite their outward success, desperately trying to make sense of it all, including some Christians. Human nature as we know it compels us to embark on an endless quest for a sense of security, belonging, purpose, achievement, recognition, etc.; we are consumed by it, yet it never seems enough. This is because humanity's quest is, in essence, a quest for identity, namely: sonship, but all the while, man has been looking in the wrong places for the wrong things. This issue goes so deep that it touches the core of our being, the foundation of our soul, i.e., what it really means to be a human.

What man lost in the Garden was not just eternal life but also the sense of identity as a 'son'. The first man, Adam, was created to be a 'son of God' [3], for he was made in the image of God [4]. When he was created, God had already prepared everything for man's needs [5]. The first-day man spent was a Sabbath, and the first thing man needed to learn was **BEING WITH GOD. That was the original meaning and purpose of man's life on earth; to walk and fellowship with God, basking in the**

Father's unconditional love and complete acceptance as a 'son'. However, that purpose was lost in the Fall.

As a result of sin, man's life on earth became cursed, as the Lord said to Adam, *"...**cursed** is the ground because of you; **in pain you shall eat of it all the days of your life**... **By the sweat of your face you shall eat bread**, till you return to the ground, for out of it you were taken; for you are dust, and to dust you shall return"* [6]. From then on, all who have borne the image of the man of dust have also borne the curse [7]. Having been expelled from home, the Garden of Eden [8], separated from the Father, the Source of Life, and excluded from the Father's ready provision, man began the lifestyle of **an orphan** and became enslaved to a lifelong quest for identity and survival.

The orphan way of life is the only way of life a natural person ever knows because he was born into it; a life filled with endless labour, fear, confusion, and hopelessness. Even Solomon, who supposedly had everything a man could ever dream of, groaned [9] *"What has a man from all the toil and striving of heart with which he toils beneath the sun? For all his days are full of sorrow, and his work is a vexation. Even in the night, his heart does not rest. This also is vanity* [10]. *As he came from his mother's womb he shall go again, naked as he came, and shall take nothing for his toil that he may carry away in his hand* [11]". This is the exact portrayal of my old life; which I came to understand after I got saved.

Since Adam, all humankind has become strangers and exiles on earth, orphans and prodigals [12]. Being accustomed to the wandering life in the world, we have long forgotten where we came from and why we were created in the first place, but the Father has NOT forgotten, and He always had a plan.

The purpose for which God sent His only begotten Son to come in the flesh was to **break the curse** in the flesh [13], so that whoever is willing to be joined to the Son may share His victory and thus **be set free from the curse** and once again live as a 'son of God' [14]. That is why Jesus told us that, as believers, we no longer have to stay under the curse conducting our lives like the orphan Gentiles who do not yet know the Father, saying, "*Do not be anxious, saying, 'What shall we eat?' or 'What shall we drink?' or 'What shall we wear?'*

For the GENTILES seek after all these things, and your heavenly Father knows that you need them all. But seek first the kingdom of God and His righteousness, and all these things will be added to you" [15].

In Christ, we can once again enter into God's REST as 'sons' like Adam did, in the beginning, intimately knowing the Father, His unconditional love, complete acceptance, and divine providence. No longer being enslaved to the maintenance of livelihood out of the fear of lack [16], and no longer striving to perform for others' affirmation. *For whoever has entered God's rest has also rested from his works as God did from His* [17].

God's eternal salvation plan is for all humanity. *He made from one man every nation of mankind to live on all the face of the earth, having determined allotted periods and the boundaries of their dwelling place, that* **they should seek God**, *and perhaps feel their way toward Him* **and find Him** [18]; that through Abraham's offspring, Jesus Christ, ALL the families of the earth may be blessed as God promised, no longer cursed [19], thus reversing the Fall; **that all may be ADOPTED by the heavenly Father through receiving the Spirit of His Son into their hearts** [20], **and as 'children of God' be RE-FATHERED and RE-MOTHERED by Him into His perfect image through the Son by the Spirit**[21].

Therefore, it can be said that the entirety of human history is a magnificent epic about exile and homecoming. This earth is not where we belong; we are just passing through. Our citizenship is in heaven [22], a city that has foundations, where we will dwell with God forever [23].

But when the fullness of time had come, God sent forth His Son, born of woman, born under the law, to redeem those who were under the law, so that **we might receive adoption as sons**. *And because you are sons,* **God has sent the Spirit of His Son into our hearts, crying, "Abba! Father!"** *So, you are* **no longer a slave, but a son**, *and if a son, then an heir through God.* (Gal 4:4-7)

For you did not receive the **spirit of slavery** *to fall back into* **fear**, *but you have received* **the Spirit of adoption** *as sons, by whom we cry,* **"Abba! Father!"** *The Spirit Himself bears witness with our spirit that* **we are children of God**. (Rom 8:15-16)

1. (Psa 139:15-16; Jer 1:5) **2.** (Rom 8:15; Gal 4:6) **3.** (Luk 3:38) **4.** (Gen 1:27) **5.** (Gen 1:29-30) **6.** (Gen 3:17-19) **7.** (1Co 15:49; Rom 5:12) **8.** (Gen 3:23-24) **9.** (2Ch 1:11-12) **10.** (Ecc 2:22-23) **11.** (Ecc 5:15) **12.** (Heb 11:13; Joh 14:18; Luk 15:11-32) **13.** (1Jn 4:2-3; Rom 8:3) **14.** (Heb 2:11-15; Rom 6:5; 8:19-23; 9:26; Gal 3:26-27) **15.** (Mat 6:31-33) **16.** (Heb 2:14-15) **17.** (Heb 4:10) **18.** (Act 17:26-27) **19.** (Gal 3:16; Gen 12:3; 18:18) **20.** (Gal 4:4-7; Rom 8:15-16) **21.** (Heb 12:5-11; Col 1:15; Rom 8:29; 2Co 3:18) **22.** (Php 3:20; Eph 2:19) **23.** (Heb 11:10; Rev 21)

ii. The Parable of The Prodigal Son

In a narrow sense, the gospel is straightforward: a father lost his son and yearned for him to return and has opened a way for it. This is depicted in 'The Parable of the Prodigal Son' [1], which most of us know well.

In the parable, the younger son asked for his share of the inheritance when his father was well and alive, and then squandered everything and put himself in dire straits. When he came to himself, he decided to return to his father and say to him, *"Father, I have sinned against heaven and before you.* **I am no longer worthy to be called your son. Treat me as one of your hired servants.***"* But while he was still a long way off, his father saw him, felt compassion, and ran, embraced, and kissed him. The father said to his servants, *"Bring quickly the best robe, and put it on him, and put a ring on his hand, and shoes on his feet. And bring the fattened calf and kill it and let us eat and* *celebrate. For **THIS MY SON** was dead, and is alive again; he was lost, and is found."*

The younger son had so much guilt and shame because of what he had done that he no longer considered himself worthy of being called a 'son'; he had thought by now, at best, he amounted to a 'servant' in his father's eyes. However, in his father's heart, he was always the son he had been yearning for day and night; it never changed a bit, regardless of what he had done. The only difference was that he was dead and lost and now is alive again and found. Hence, upon seeing him from a distance, the father ran to him and embraced and kissed him as a father would a son.

Since *all have sinned and fall short of the glory of God* [2], it can be said that every single person on earth is a prodigal son whom the heavenly Father yearns for. Remember, before 'The Parable of the Prodigal Son', Jesus also told 'The Parable of the Lost Sheep' and 'The Parable of the Lost Coin' [3].

Together they reveal one truth about our Father in heaven: **every single one is precious to Him**, so precious that He would be willing to sacrifice His only begotten Son, who shares eternal oneness and glory with Him, allowing Him to be humiliated, crucified and separated from Him, for the sake of only one sinner, to bring that lost son back home[4]. It is beyond our human comprehension that the almighty, holy, glorious God, the Creator of the universe, can love us and love us so much that He suffers from the excruciating pain of heartbrokenness. In view of those brought forth by Him who are separated from Him by sin, He would do everything, even the unthinkable, to bring us all back to Him. As Isaiah 49:15-16 says, *"Can a woman forget her nursing child, that she should have no compassion on the son of her womb?* **Even these may forget, yet I will not forget you.** *Behold, I have engraved you on the palms of My hands..."*. Having loved and brought us into being, the Father loves us to the end.

Moreover, we see in the story that contrary to the younger son's self-assessment of no longer being worthy of being called a 'son', the father addressed him as **'this my son'** before the servants and ordered them to put the best robe on him, a ring on his hand, and shoes on his feet, to restore to him the honour and dignity that belong to a son, and also kill the fattened calf to celebrate. Jesus told us that the angels of God in heaven celebrate the homecoming of one prodigal [5].

This seems like a happy ending. However, from the Bible, we know that the story did not end there; Jesus went on to talk about the older son.

The older son was angry when he heard that his younger brother had returned and that his father had killed the fattened calf for him. He told his father, who implored him, "**Look, these many years I have served you, and I never disobeyed your command, yet you never gave me a young goat**, that I might celebrate with my friends. But *when this son of yours came, who has devoured your property with prostitutes, you killed the fattened calf for him!'* The father said to him, "**SON, you are always with me, and all that is mine is yours.** *It was fitting to celebrate and be glad, for this your brother was dead, and is alive; he was lost, and is found."*

The father never loved the older brother any less; he also addressed him as '**son**', and said to him that '*all that is mine is yours*'. Yet, despite being home with his father all this time, he did not really understand his father's heart towards him, nor his own identity as a 'son'. Whereas with a contrite heart, the younger son, upon returning, asked his father to treat him as a servant, the older son by then had already been conducting his life in the likeness of a 'servant' for many years, seeing his relationship with his father as contractual, one that was about performance and reward. Not recognising that the simple fact of being a 'son' already entitled him to all that his father had, let alone a young goat. He projected his distorted view of his relationship with his father onto his younger brother and felt his Father was unfair.

It may be said that the older son, though always at the father's house, was AN ORPHAN at heart.

The older son in the parable is typically interpreted as the law-observing Jews who have connected with the God of Abraham, Isaac, and Jacob since ancient times, and the younger son is all who come to the Father through repentance and faith in Jesus Christ by grace. However, it may be said that **the older son also represents Christian believers who have become members of the household of God yet are stuck in the orphan way of life, continuing in the old quest for identity and security**. At one level, Jesus was contrasting grace with works; at another level, He highlighted a heart condition that believers are often subject to, affecting how we relate to the heavenly Father.

Grow In Sonship

Just as the children of Israel came out of Egypt, yet Egypt (with its idolatrous way of life) did not come out of them, all believers as adopted orphans suffer a 'sequela' from our past ordeal, that is, because of **our old self**, despite receiving the Spirit of adoption as sons, we do not begin to think or act like 'sons' overnight, even though we know it in our head and declare it with our mouth. The Bible does not tell us what life was like for the younger son after returning home and that joyous celebration. I imagine it would take a while for him to adapt to the lifestyle of a 'son' again and be rid of all the orphan habits that he picked up while straying. In my personal walk, I have discovered that to go from a 'prodigal son' to a 'son of God', there is a whole 'JOURNEY OF REHABILITATION' that all believers are called to participate in and being born again in Jesus Christ only commences that journey.

In addition to believing in Jesus and having our sin cleansed by His precious blood, the gospel, in a broad sense, also includes man's total restoration through sanctification.

FULL RESTORATION is what the Father had in mind when He sent His Son to die for us. The complete reinstatement of the stature of a son, not in name only, is why the father in the parable did not simply receive the prodigal back. He went further to order the servants to dress him up in the attire fit for a son and kill the fattened calf to celebrate in his honour.

The whole 'good news' is that in Christ, not only can we have a right standing before God, but we can also be conformed to the image of the Son through sanctification, attaining to the measure of the stature of the fullness of Christ, so that He might, in a very real sense, be the firstborn among many brothers [6].

However, it may be said that we often conduct ourselves as if returning home as a prodigal is the end of the story, and the rest is just ploughing through life. Also, sometimes after coming to the house of God as the 'prodigal son', instead of maturing towards the stature of the Son of God, we go on to become the 'older son'...

1. (Luk 15:11-32) 2. (Rom 3:23) 3. (Luk 15:1-10) 4. (Joh 10:16; 17:21-24)
5. (Luk 15:7,10) 6. (Eph 4:13; Rom 8:29)

iii. A Personal Testimony

Since becoming a Christian, it has been a long journey of being 'detoxed' of the orphan spirit and growing in sonship, and I am still in that process.

An orphan trait typically does not disappear overnight. One of the orphan traits I have had to battle with is striving to perform, which I know is familiar to many. Highly prized by the world, which thrives on our being performance-driven, it is the very thing that testified that the older son in the parable could not yet truly relate to his father as a son. From constantly being compared with cousins and family friends' children by parents, with classmates by teachers, to having our exam marks published on a school wall in the order of high to low with our names next to them, Chinese children grow up in a brutally competitive environment. 'Outdoing others' is how we have been programmed – survival of the fittest, and I was at the top of this game. When we were wandering orphans in the

Grow In Sonship

world, we learnt from the world how to survive, and having learnt how to survive, we carry on operating out of survival mode even when we are back at the Father's house. Such has been my struggle. What once was my greatest strength became my greatest weakness.

Having been brought up to be competitive and aspiring to worldly success, even after I became born-again, for a long time, I still could not help but compare myself with others on worldly terms. I have always known that I have a calling to the Christian ministry. Preparing for that calling means the Lord is taking my life on a completely different path than what otherwise would have been pursuing worldly ambitions.

However, while my worldly passions and endeavours ran out of steam, my performance-driven old self sometimes aroused a sense of jealousy and failure. *My peers have moved on; some have been promoted to senior positions with polished careers; some have established successful businesses and accumulated considerable wealth; some have married the rich and are living luxurious lifestyles... What have I accomplished? Oh, I am so lagging behind.* I wrestled with those thoughts. The Lord was relentless in killing my ego and propensity for worldly performance. He brought me from a high-flying, well-paid, glamorous international investment banking job down to a back-office role at a domestic, commercial bank doing what I deemed monotonous tasks where almost all my qualifications, credentials, and other learnt skills became irrelevant. He brought me from the stature of the 'goddess of excellence', whom others used to envy and look up to, down to a byword for failure and stupidity, an object of ridicule and scorn, to the same people. I had to face so much shame in the family and among relatives and friends...

But every time I considered how the King of kings and Lord of lords has loved me from eternity and abandoned His throne in heaven to

come to earth to lay down His life for me, deep down, I knew that He is worth my everything. And as I reflected on how God chose the uneducated lowly fishermen and not the wise and powerful to start His Church, it became increasingly clear to me that worldly achievements amount to very little in God's eyes [1]. Thus, I found myself offering my life at the altar, again and again, saying, "Lord, I am willing to be a fool for You [2], for You are infinitely worthy."

While withdrawing identity from worldly things is obviously necessary, the need to withdraw identity from spiritual things is subtler yet equally essential. **Out of the unhealed orphan heart, we can easily swap 'worldly performance' for 'spiritual performance'**, being obsessively concerned with, for instance, how knowledgeable or pious we appear to others, how well our giftings are recognised, how much our services are appreciated, how big or lively our congregation is, how many are following our ministries, how popular our sermons, books or songs are, and so on. These, despite their spiritual associations, can all still be performances for men. I myself am not immune; I carried my old performance-driven way of being into my church life, particularly in prophetic gifting.

I have always been fascinated by revelatory gifting and surrounded by prophetic people, some of whom operate at very high levels of seer anointing. Since for a long time, I could not see pictures or visions like they did, and especially, I never saw the Lord Jesus, whom I love so dearly; for years, I felt self-conscious and inferior. At times, I wondered if the Lord loved me less... This continued until one day; the Lord reminded me of a prayer that I prayed when I was two years into the Christian faith. I said, "Lord, please don't give me anything that would destroy me." Little did I know the Lord took it seriously. He showed me that if He opened my spiritual eyes, I would immediately take identity in it and become puffed up.

Then I realised that the real issue was not my ability to see into the spirit realm. Still, my need to use that as a means to alleviate the sense of insecurity that sprung from my orphan heart and the false belief of that being a measure of spirituality. This urge to cover our insecurity with a recognisable ability to make ourselves look more acceptable to others applies to any natural and spiritual gifting. I repented. I decided to keep loving the Lord even if I was never to see a thing or be deemed the least gifted person in my Christian circle.

Over time, I overcame idolatry towards prophetic seeing, and my love for the Lord increasingly deepened despite not being able to behold Him visually [3]. Then, one day, the Lord manifested Himself to me in a dream [4]. I was amazed that it felt like we had known each other and been seeing each other all along; the intimacy shared between us in the dream felt the same as when I was awake. Since then, I have encountered the Lord quite a number of times.

Nevertheless, I would be a liar if I claimed to have overcome entirely in that area. **Our old self is very stubborn, and the 'journey of rehabilitation' has multiple layers.** If I am honest, insecurity still pops up every now and then, especially in corporate settings. *Why is everyone else getting words and pictures, but I am not? Shall I give one anyway; perhaps it's harmless to give a general encouraging word? How come their prophetic giftings are fancier than mine? How come they are getting all the attention? Shall I give a 'wow' word to outdo them?* Though seldom articulated, this type of feeling sometimes surges up, and I suspect possibly the same for many people with giftings of any sort.

Like the older brother in the parable who compared himself with his younger brother, in the church, we often subconsciously compare ourselves with others in various aspects.

Precisely because, like the older son, we still carry the orphan heart; we still have not found total rest in the Father's unconditional love and complete acceptance. Then, unconsciously, we flood the church with teachings and prophecies tainted by striving hearts and do works out of rivalry [5], and our spiritually disguised worldliness continually causes disunity in the body [6].

Oh Lord, deliver us from the orphan spirit; deliver us from the way of the world!

Whenever the above happens, it reminds me that I am still a work in progress! I need more healing! So, I would intentionally choose to love my brothers and sisters by allowing them the opportunities to shine, listen to what God is saying through them, learn from them, and make up my mind to speak only what and when the Lord wants me to [7]. Thank God, I am getting better at it.

Grow In Sonship

The journey of growing in sonship has different stages; the further we go, the steeper and narrower it gets. While recognising we are sons of God in Christ and overcoming the orphan traits here and there as we go through life are good, to build our entire life based on our relationship with the Father while in the world is much more challenging because there is nothing else to fall back on. Our ultimate goal here is to reverse the consequence of the Fall and go back to the Garden. This means **we need to relearn the lifestyle of totally depending on God and revolving our lives around Him** like Adam and Eve were in the beginning. The grace of God will empower us to do so, so long as we are willing. God's restoration plan for humankind is radical. Who would have thought He would send His own Son to die for us? So, if we choose to adhere to His plan fully, we too, would appear a bit radical. It will sometimes feel like you are going against the whole world.

Grow In Sonship

Since heeding the call of the Lord to serve Him full-time, I have left everything behind, all that the world has to offer, including financial security, to follow Him wherever He leads and do whatever He commands. Such a lifestyle is against everything I have been raised to believe and is certainly unheard of in the culture and society I come from, but undoubtedly not strange in church history [8]. I have met much criticism and scepticism from family, relatives, and friends in and outside the church. While some are genuinely concerned for me, some are waiting to see a spectacular fall. I wish I could say that I am always strong in the faith, but the truth is that there have been times when fears overtook me, and I succumbed to the taunts of the enemy, and the temptation is to **begin to seek validation and identity in what I do for God**.

Using writing the *Mystery of Sanctification* series as an example: I started with much excitement, but gradually I became anxious and perturbed about how it was going to turn out, seeing that it is the first major project I have embarked on since choosing the ministry path against the warnings of many, and all eyes are watching. *Who am I to write books? Some people are way more qualified than me. Who would be interested? If the sale is poor, I will look like a total failure to those who are sceptical. They will mock me, saying, "See, I told you!"* At times, doubts brew like dark clouds over my head and quickly roll in like a storm, and I become worried not only about the books but also about my life and future, everything! In no time, I am drowned in the tears of self-pity. Only as I once again **die to the outward success of the works of God**, shafts of light would pierce through the darkness, and peace return. "Even if I am deemed a failure by the whole world, I still have to follow You and do what You say, and if I perish, I perish[9]." I said to the Lord in moments of surrender. And He always comforted me, saying, "He who trusts in the Lord will never be put to shame."

Grow In Sonship

Finally, the deepest hidden striving that I am learning to overcome is the pursuit of spiritual maturity. How can pursuing spiritual maturity go wrong? Yes, it can. How can a toddler run like Usain Bolt? Such is the pressure I sometimes put on myself because of my performance-oriented upbringing. Just like natural bodily growth takes time, spiritual growth also takes time. It requires us to live through life experiences that cannot be hurried. However, when one strives to become mature out of the flesh, he would either be conceited on account of his maturity, which is not so mature, or excessively self-critical on account of his weaknesses. I confess I have swung to both sides of the pendulum before.

Once, I was beating myself up for something I messed up. Presenting my weaknesses and failure before the Father, I groaned, "Look, I'm so far from being like You", and tears started trickling down. But I heard the Father say to me, "I'm committed to your restoration. It is my desire that you are fully healed and restored, and I'm committed to it." I knew He said so to take the pressure off me. Indeed, I felt comforted. Then for the first time, I sensed the pain in the Father's heart because of the disruption caused by the Fall to His communion with His children, all whom He has made, and His determination to restore it. I wept.

Today, I am learning to become more like a child as Jesus taught us [10], for a child is not overly concerned with his maturity. Still, he simply heartily enjoys his relationship with the Father, knowing His love and acceptance are a given.

In fact, if I were to summarise the 'journey of rehabilitation' using one sentence, it is **learning to become like a child again**. The world we grow up in hurries us into adulthood; it signals us to become capable and savvy as early as we can, as much as we can [11]. Then, like Adam and Eve, out of self-consciousness used fig leaves to cover their nakedness [12], we go on to collect and deck ourselves with all kinds of accolades to cover our insecurity.

Growing in sonship, however, is returning to the innocence and simplicity of being known and loved by the Father, daily walking in His delight, and knowing Him and loving Him back with the same love He has loved us.

It takes 'downsizing', stripping off the 'fig leaves' of all shapes and forms that we have put on, and unlearning the ways of the world to become like a child again, such that we can stand before the Father 'naked' yet not ashamed [13], knowing that we are already completely accepted by Him, the whole package.

From a life that was all about performance and striving for the praise of men to a life of only desiring to become more like Him and do His will before going home to be with Him forever, it really has been a journey. Dear friends, how I wish I had the words to describe the riches that I have found in my beloved Lord Jesus, such that the world has paled into insignificance, such that I no longer feel the need to boast according to the flesh, though, like Paul, I have a reason for confidence in the flesh. *But whatever gain I had, I counted as loss for the sake of Christ. Indeed, I count everything as loss because of the surpassing worth of knowing Christ Jesus my Lord. For His sake, I am willing to suffer the loss of all things and count them as rubbish, in order that I may gain Christ* [14]. How I wish I had the words to express the FREEDOM and REST that I have found in the Father, even in my work-in-progress state, knowing that I am completely loved and accepted by Him and that I can approach the throne of grace whenever to snuggle up to Him quietly as a little child [15]. Even if I never achieve a thing in this life, even if I become the scum of the world, the refuse of all things [16]. And that I am free to be whom the Father has created me to be – I have no desire to be anyone else – and walk into the destiny He has designated for me.

Grow In Sonship

TRULY, IN THE SPIRITUAL SENSE, THE FATHER IS THE GARDEN OF EDEN, AND THE SON THE TREE OF LIFE.

Mankind is created in such a way that we feel most FULFILLED when we 'LIVE and MOVE and HAVE OUR BEING in God [17], who is our Garden, our home.

When we 'live' in God, we find the reason for our existence – to be in a relationship with the Creator, or else we may find life in this world meaningless, hopeless, lonely, and depressing, and some might even have suicidal thoughts. When we 'have our being' in God, we find OUR IDENTITY AS SONS, much loved and cared for by our heavenly Father, or else we would be carrying the orphan heart, struggling with insecurity and anxiety, and exhausted from striving. When we 'move' in God, we find our purpose and calling as individuals and step into the wonderful plans the Father has for our lives, or else we are likely to be enslaved to making a living out of the fear of lack, feeling bound and suffocating.

I have shaky days, but generally speaking, today, I feel at home and at rest wherever I am. That is because I am back in my eternal home, THE GARDEN OF EDEN, partaking in THE TREE OF LIFE. **Just as the Son is in the Father and the Father in the Son, the Son is in me and I in Them, now and forever** [18].

I know this 'journey of rehabilitation' goes on. As I go through different seasons in life, I will continue to be transformed. In this journey, I may stumble and make mistakes, but I know what I can always fall back on – the unconditional love and complete acceptance of my Father in heaven.

Over the years, I have come across different interpretations of what it means to walk in sonship. For example, some consider it an automatic reality or process after receiving Jesus Christ as the

Saviour; some equate it to exercising certain gifts of the Spirit or carrying out a particular aspect of the Christian ministry; still, some interpret it as being wrapped up and loved up in God's presence. I understand that walking in sonship in whatever shape or form has to result in REAL RENEWAL in us.

Sonship implies a relationship, and the other side of such a relationship is the fatherhood of God, and the nature of 'fathering' is reproducing one's image in another. As shared in the first book, *Last Eve*, the Greek word for 'father' **patér** (Strong's: G3962), according to HELPS Word-studies, means 'one who imparts life and is committed to it; a progenitor, bringing into being to pass on the potential for likeness'. Therefore, to grow in sonship is to be transformed into the image of God the Father, whose image is fully embodied and revealed in Jesus Christ, the Son of God [19], whose image is formed in us through sanctification[20], which is conditional on our continually and intentionally choosing to live according to God's ways. The outcome of such should be the deep, unwavering ASSURANCE of the Father's love and acceptance within, the healing and restoration of the soul, and the growth of the spirit man that bears the Father's image through the Son. The outward manifestation of such can be summarised in one word – LOVE – loving God and loving others. As it is written, *"Love is from God, and **whoever loves has been BORN OF GOD and knows God**. Anyone who does not love does not know God, because **GOD IS LOVE**"* [21]. Each tree is known by its fruit [22].

---

1. (1Co 1:26-29) **2.** (1Co 4:10) **3.** (1Pe 1:8) **4.** (Joh 14:21) **5.** (Eze 13:1,17; Mar 7:21-23; Php 1:15) **6.** (Jas 4:1-4) **7.** (Joh 7:18) **8.** (Mar 10:21,28-29; Act 2:44-45; 4:32-37) **9.** (Est 4:16) **10.** (Mat 18:2-3) **11.** (Luk 16:8) **12.** (Gen 3:7) **13.** (Gen 2:25) **14.** (Php 3:4-8) **15.** (Heb 4:16) **16.** (1Co 4:13) **17.** (Act 17:28) **18.** (Joh 17:21,23) **19.** (Joh 14:9; 2Co 4:4; Col 1:15). **20.** (Gal 4:19; 2Co 3:18; Col 3:10) **21.** (1Jn 4:7-8) **22.** (Luk 6:43-44)

iv. An Exhortation from The Author

Proverbs 29:18 (KJV) says, "*Where there is no vision, the people perish.*" If we are not clear about where we come from, where we are going, and the purpose of our lives on earth, we will run aimlessly. If we cannot distinguish that which is eternal from that which is temporal, we will box as one beating the air [1], wasting our time and energy on things that will eventually pass away. **THE ETERNAL PERSPECTIVE should determine how we live our lives on earth.** In light of man's Fall and exile from Eden and the way back home opened by the Cross, I believe that the purpose of man's life on earth is first to find God through Jesus Christ [2], and having found Him, use well the time left to be restored and sanctified and grow into mature manhood as a son.

Our lives on earth, with their twists and turns, serve to uncover the areas of our brokenness and, therefore, best allow us to be healed and attain the

Grow In Sonship

measure of the stature of the fullness of Christ. Eventually, bearing the glorious image of the Father, we, as the sons of God, will be revealed to all creation [3]. And I believe that with an eternal testimony of overcoming [4], man's latter glory shall be greater than the former. However, we only have so much time on earth; remember, it is a race! [5] I wasted so many years as an orphan chasing after and building my life on that which will ultimately be destroyed [6]. I now know better; hence for the rest of my time in the flesh, I only want to live for that which has eternal significance [7].

What about you, my friend?

*And I heard a loud voice from the thron saying, "Behold, **the dwelling place of God is with man. He will dwell with them**, and they will be His people, and God Himself will be with them as their God. He will wipe away every tear from their eyes, and death shall be no more, neither shall there be mourning, nor crying, nor pain anymore, for **the former things have passed away**." And He who was seated on the throne said, "Behold, **I am making all things new**... To the thirsty I will give from the spring of the water of life without payment. **THE ONE WHO CONQUERS** will have this heritage, and **I will be his God and HE WILL BE MY SON**.* (Rev 21:3-7)

---

1. (2Co 4:18; 1Co 9:26) **2.** (Act 17:26-27; Mat 7:8; 1Ch 28:9) **3.** (Rom 8:19) **4.** (Rev 21:7) **5.** (1Co 9:24; 2Ti 4:7; Heb 12:1) **6.** (Heb 12:26-29; 2Pe 3:7; Rev 21:1; 1Co 13:8-10) **7.** (1Pe 4:2)

III.

The Sanctification in The Family

i. The Redemption of Family

Overcoming the orphan spirit is a process and, most likely, a lifelong journey. It is God's heart that as we go through different seasons and circumstances in life, every part of us that falls short of the glory of God would be exposed and refined, and every wound examined and healed so that we would continually grow in sonship. Within such a process, personally, the turning point since which I truly began to know what the heavenly Father is like and develop an intimate relationship with Him and enter His rest was when I started going through the sanctification in the family being healed of family wounds.

The Sanctification in The Family

Since receiving the revelation of the Lord Jesus being my Bridegroom in the early years, I have been continually walking in the bridal realm persevering through various trials in life, whereby my relationship with the Lord continues to deepen. Today, I am blessed to know the Lord Jesus intimately, deeply acquainted with His 'frequency' (i.e., a specific impression in the spirit that distinguishes Him from anything or anyone else), and how He is towards me. I feel very free with Him, knowing I am fully known and much loved by Him. (The bridal revelation is primarily expounded in *Last Eve*, the first book of the *Mystery of Sanctification* series.) While being accustomed to the bliss of fellowshipping with the Son for many years, fellowshipping with the Father was a relatively unfamiliar paradigm to me. I used to always commune with Jesus, seldom the Father, until I had a spiritual encounter one day. During a season of experiencing family-related inner healing, I sensed Jesus standing on my right earnestly gesturing me to go forward to where the Father was seated, and simultaneously, I heard in the spirit, "***The Father Himself loves you***" [1]

Whereas positionally, I was reconciled with the Father upon believing in Jesus and becoming born-again, relationally, I was formally introduced to the Father by the Son for the first time.

There began my journey of being **re-fathered** and **re-mothered** by the heavenly Father. I subsequently discovered that I was a broken individual and that many of my initial impressions of the Father were wrong (hence, the uneasiness to relate to Him). And that was mainly due to the experience of my strict upbringing and the resulting perceptions of my earthly father and mother, whom I subconsciously used as a reference for the heavenly Father.

Despite many stories of parental failure, I still believe that many fathers and mothers in this world share a beautiful trait, a trait that mirrors the very heart of the heavenly Father, and that is, they hope their children can go further and higher than themselves in life and would even make sacrifices in their own lives to help them achieve that.

I know the Chinese parents are particularly adamant about this, and among all the Chinese parents I know, mine went above and beyond. Through their many great sacrifices, my father and mother let me step on their backs and stand on their shoulders and lifted me onto a plateau of new possibilities in life that they never had the luxury to experience; they afforded me the opportunities to broaden my horizons to see more and know more than they were ever able to. I am wholeheartedly thankful for all that my parents have done for me. They have been a blessing to my life and will always be. If raising the next generation to go further and higher is God's mandate for all fathers and mothers, then mine fulfilled their part to the best of their knowledge and ability.

The Sanctification in The Family

While this might be the reality with our parents in the natural, this is also meant to be the case in the spiritual. The next generation is meant to carry on the baton and continue to build on the spiritual legacy of the previous generation so that from generation to generation, it goes from glory to glory in terms of spiritual advancement. However, it may be said that compared to the natural, the outworking of such in the spiritual has primarily been hindered. Because *all have sinned and fall short of the glory of God*[2], parents tend to pass down their brokenness alongside good traits. Mine were not exempt. In pushing me hard to attain what they were deprived of in life, I became broken.

Family can be a tricky place. Those we love and are supposed to love us most often happen to be the ones who hurt us most, and vice versa. Other than unforeseen tragedies, **the fallen nature** that has been following us since that first disobedience in the Garden has contributed to countless broken marriages and families and, ultimately, broken individuals. I am lucky that my parents' marriage is intact and that I had input from both of them growing up. Nonetheless, because they are imperfect, their disciplining as it seemed best to them still broke me [3], let alone those who sadly grow up in a dysfunctional family or toxic environment, missing a father or mother or both, or under an abusive parent(s).

Whether it is rejection, neglect, abandonment, absence, or abuse, the pain of family wounds is unspeakable yet so real. We carry it daily, consciously or unconsciously. It affects our well-being, life choices, relationships with God and other human beings, and everything we do, regardless of our culture. In some parts of the world, we may get away with openly dishonouring or even cursing our fathers and mothers out of our pain. In some other parts of the world, fathers and mothers are elevated to such high status, as if they are infallible, any wrong is justifiable, and any questioning is disrespectful, also sometimes with a

The Sanctification in The Family

sensationalised myth that fathers and mothers are unfailingly utterly selfless. In the former case, we express our pain unrestrainedly while continually hurting and antagonising our parents. In the latter case, we routinely cover and suppress our pain while forgetting the biblical truth that our fathers and mothers, too, are broken sinners [4]. Neither of these helps with our healing. Explicitly or implicitly, there is a chasm between our hearts and our fathers' and mothers'.

Family is very dear to God's heart because God Himself is a Father, and we all come from Him [5]. The last verse of the last book of the Old Testament conveys a profound longing of the Father's heart: *turn the hearts of fathers to their children and the hearts of children to their fathers* [6], and ultimately, turn all the hearts of the sons of man back to Him, the Father of all [7].

Seizing upon unfortunate life circumstances and the brokenness of our fathers and mothers, whom we commonly subconsciously use as a reference for the heavenly Father, the devil has tried very hard to smear and pervert the image of the Father. But the Father seeks to be known by all His children as He is. As a matter of fact, **Jesus came to reveal the Father** [8], even one of His names is called 'EverlastingFather'[9]. **Our heavenly Father desires to father and mother us in the areas where we have never been fathered or mothered, and RE-FATHER and RE-MOTHER us in the areas where our earthly fathers and mothers fall short**. He wants to show us what He is like as a perfect Parent, to remedy the painful history, so that we might be comforted, healed and made whole, genuinely able to enjoy the FREEDOM and REST as sons, grow into His image, and walk into all the good plans He has for us.

Particularly, in Christ, the Father has granted us the grace to have the strength to crucify the chief culprit, the sinful, fallen nature we inherited from our forefathers, and instead, take on His divine nature [10]. By our overcoming, we can pull down those generational strongholds and free our children and our children's children once and for all from the generational patterns of sins that have been recurring in the family line. Also, our partaking in God's divine nature to whatever maximum degree while we are on earth can become a spiritual inheritance that we leave to our posterity, each generation building on the legacy of the previous one.

1. (Joh 16:27) **2.** (Rom 3:23) **3.** (Heb 12:10) **4.** (Rom 3:23) **5.** (Eph 3:14-15) **6.** (Mal 4:6) **7.** (Eph 4:6) **8.** (Joh 1:18; 14:7,9; 17:6) **9.** (Isa 9:6) **10.** (2Pe 1:3-4)

ii. The Spiritual Umbilical Cord

A family comes from a marriage; in every marriage, the wife is someone's daughter, and the husband is someone's son. The Scripture says, "***A man shall LEAVE his father and his mother** and hold fast to his wife, and they shall become one flesh*" [1]. The 'leave' here is not just physically moving out of the parents' house to move in with the spouse. The Hebrew word for 'leave' **azab** (Strong's: H5800), according to Strong's Exhaustive Concordance, means 'to loosen'. Perhaps this can be better understood with the picture of an umbilical cord that attaches to every new-born baby.

While in the womb, through the umbilical cord, the mother's body supplies oxygenated, nutrient-rich blood to the baby, but once the baby is born, the umbilical cord has to be cut. Whereas the physical cord is cut shortly after the birth, it can be said that in the spirit, there remains a 'spiritual umbilical cord' that attaches us to our earthly mother, who is also one flesh with our earthly father through their marriage. **This spiritual umbilical cord is cut through sanctification, which is an intentional process.** Ezekiel 16:3-4 (NASB) describes the natural state of the man born of flesh and blood before being sanctified [2]: *"Your origin and your birth are from the land of the Canaanite, your father was an Amorite and your mother a Hittite.* ***As for your birth, on the day you were born your navel cord was not cut...".***

If the spiritual umbilical cords have not been cut, then though a man and woman get married, they actually have not yet 'left' or 'be loosened' from their respective fathers and mothers, who, in turn, would be passing on their sinful nature/lusts of the flesh/sinful tendencies along with the generational struggles in full force, even when the husband and wife have been born again. Consequently, they bring the flesh from their respective families into the marriage, which then becomes a double whammy, for, in sharing 'one flesh', one has to deal

The Sanctification in The Family

with two persons' flesh instead of one's own! No wonder married couples sometimes complain and reminisce about their single days: "I was totally fine when I was by myself until you turned up, and the problems came with you!" The flesh brought into the marriage from both sides of the families, if uncrucified, hinders the husband and wife's souls from becoming more and more one, and unfortunately, in some cases, can lead to the parting of the two souls, i.e., divorce.

Cutting the spiritual umbilical cords essentially deals with the flesh at the source. Though it does not rid a person of all fleshly struggles, it does help overcome those major inherited ones and help the person to be set apart from his blood family. Remember, Jesus said, *"Do not think that I have come to bring peace to the earth.* **I have** *not* **come to bring** *peace, but* **A SWORD**. *For I have come* **to set a man against his father, and a daughter against her mother, and a daughter-in-law against her mother-in-law"** [3].

Moreover, suppose a husband and wife have not cut their spiritual umbilical cords. In that case, they will continue to pass down the flesh they have inherited from their fathers and mothers to the next generation via the spiritual umbilical cords attached to their children. **Without the intentional intervention of sanctification, the same flesh would perpetuate in a family line through generations of interconnected spiritual umbilical cords. Therefore, it leaves each generation of carriers prone to the same types of sins (though not entirely unavoidable due to the existence of human will), thus allowing the enemy to form generational strongholds in the family.** That is why we often see repeating patterns of sins manifest in one generation after another.

For example, the Bible shows that deceit recurred generationally along Abraham's family line. Abraham first lied to Pharaoh and then Abimelech, king of Gerar, about Sarah, his wife, saying she was his sister [4]. His son Isaac did precisely the same

The Sanctification in The Family

thing; he lied to the men of Gerar and Abimelech, king of the Philistines, about Rebekah, his wife, saying that she was his sister[5]. Jacob deceived Esau and stole his birthright [6]. Jacob's eleven sons lied to their father about what they did to Joseph [7]. Similarly, lust was an issue in David's family. David himself had many wives and committed adultery with Bathsheba [8]. His son Amnon raped his half-sister Tamar [9]. His son and successor Solomon loved many foreign women; he had 700 wives and 300 concubines who eventually turned his heart away from the Lord [10].

The first Adam was created to be a living soul in the image and likeness of God [11]. However, because of the Fall, man became susceptible to fleshly lusts (the sinful nature taken on in the body), which war against the soul [12]. Yielding to the sinful nature passed down in all the families of the earth rather than ruling over it, generation after generation, men, continually sin against God and one another[13], resulting in a sea of broken souls...

Among such, when a child is sinned against by his father or/and mother during his formative years, the cuts go particularly deep. Without sanctification and the healing released through it, one could be carrying such wounds for the rest of his life, and when they become parents with the same flesh, they are likely to go on to break their children…

But thanks be to God! The Son of God came with a nature like our sinful nature, yet did not sin [14]. Now if the Spirit of the Son dwells within us [15],

> then not only have we been imputed Christ's righteousness (i.e., the so-called 'justification by faith'), but in Christ, we have also been granted the grace to no longer walk according to the flesh, that is, yielding to the sinful nature, as we once did, but to walk according to the Spirit, that is, obeying God's righteousness, leading to sanctification [16].

The Sanctification in The Family

The last Adam became a life-giving spirit [17]. Upon being born again, the Spirit comes to dwell in our heart and becomes one with our spirit man [18]. Then the sanctification process starts, whose progress depends on our willingness to continually present our members to God as instruments for righteousness as opposed to sin, that is, intentionally choosing to conduct ourselves in accordance with God's words, whether written or spoken, rather than yielding to fleshly lusts, in all the life circumstances orchestrated and presented by the Spirit by grace [19].

Each time, responding to our willingness and determination to deny a fleshly lust in an area in a specific circumstance, the Spirit by grace would empower us to resist and eventually crucify the flesh with its lust, putting to death the old self with its sinful nature in that particular area to a certain degree [20]. Over time, as we put off more and more the old self with its sinful nature, correspondingly, we would put on more and more the new self, the spirit man that progressively grows into the image and stature of Christ[21], who is the image of God [22], thereby partaking more and more in God's divine nature and becoming more and more sanctified. During this process, the Spirit also releases healing to our soul, increasingly restoring it to WHOLENESS [23]. (I will explain sanctification in detail in another book of the *Mystery of Sanctification* series.)

Again, using the umbilical cord analogy, in addition to the existing spiritual umbilical cord that attaches us to our earthly father and mother, when we become born-again, we receive another spiritual umbilical cord that connects us to our heavenly Father. So now we have two inputs: the sinful nature through the fleshly umbilical cord and God's divine nature through the heavenly umbilical cord. These are opposed to each other, as the Word says, *"The flesh lusts against the Spirit, and the Spirit against the flesh; and these are contrary to one another..."* [24].

The Sanctification in The Family

Regardless of whether or not we are aware of this umbilical cord dynamic/the reality of inherited flesh, as believers, we are supposed to deal with an area of sinful nature as it becomes exposed, i.e., repent and align ourselves to God's righteous words whenever we are convicted by the Holy Spirit of a specific sin. Gradually, we crucify more and more flesh and become more and more sanctified. If we do this, we are already experiencing renewal and altering our family histories' trajectories, which is superb! Meanwhile, for some of us, especially those whose fathers and mothers are still around, there could also be a season(s) focused on cutting the fleshly umbilical cord, experiencing sanctification in the family in a more concentrated, intense way. Through such a season, I pulled down some generational strongholds in my family, came to know the Father intimately, reconciled with my parents in the heart, and became healed of family wounds. Next, I will share my experience of such a season with you.

The Sanctification in The Family

My experience does not reflect all realities of family situations, nor is it sufficient to answer all family-related issues in their varying nature and degrees of severity and complexity. However, in whatever way and to whatever extent, you might identify with this part of my journey of sanctification; in sharing it, I wish to bring you hope of healing and wholeness.

1. (Gen 2:24; Mat 19:5; Eph 5:31) **2.** (Joh 3:6) **3.** (Mat 10:34-35) **4.** (Gen 12:11-20; 20:2-18) **5.** (Gen 26:6-11) **6.** (Gen 25:29-34) **7.** (Gen 37:18-35) **8.** (2Sa 11) **9.** (2Sa 13:1-22) **10.** (1Ki 11:1-8) **11.** (Gen 1:27; 2:7, KJV; 5:1; 1Co 15:45, KJV) **12.** (1Pe 2:11, KJV) **13.** (Gen 4:6-7, NKJV; Jas 1:14-15) **14.** (Rom 8:3, GNT; Heb 4:15) **15.** (Gal 4:6) **16.** (Eph 2:1-3; Rom 6:14,19; 8:1-17, NKJV) **17.** (1Co 15:45, NASB) **18.** (1Co 6:17) **19.** (Rom 6:12-13,19) **20.** (Gal 5:24; Rom 6:6) **21.** (Eph 4:22,24; 2Co 3:18; Col 3:9-10; 1Co 15:49) **22.** (2Co 4:4; Col 1:15) **23.** (Psa 23:3; 41:4, KJV) **24.** (Gal 5:17, NKJV)

iii. Overcoming in The Family

You may recall what I shared at the beginning of Chapter II, how I, seeking to please my parents, became that 'perfect kid' excelling in almost everything yet struggling inside. Not knowing anything better back then, this is how I dealt with it: I ran away from home. When I was 17, there was an opportunity to go to England to study. I took it and never looked back because I desperately wanted to start afresh, to have my own freedom without my parents constantly watching. After I arrived in the UK, I did not call my parents very often; it was the last thing on my mind. Whenever I visited home, about once a year, there would be acrimony, arguments, and tears. This went on even after I became a Christian.

In 2010, my parents came to the UK to attend my university graduation ceremony. At that time, I introduced them to a Christian couple, my cell group leaders, who sort of 'adopted' me. In the

The Sanctification in The Family

middle of a barbecue at their house, all of a sudden, mum started weeping. The Christian lady and my aunt escorted my mum to a room at the back. Afterward, I was told that mum was heartbroken because she saw that I was closer to the Christian lady than herself, even though she had sacrificed so much to support my overseas studies. With aunt's help in translation, the lady, who knew why I struggled in my relationship with my parents, told my mum the secret that I had kept all those years, that I was very hurt by their constant pressure on me to perform when I was growing up.

After my parents returned to their hotel, I stayed at the Christian couple's place. The lady said to me, "Shan, have a good night of sleep, and tomorrow morning, go to your parents and say 'sorry' to them." I said, "I'll pray about it." However, in my heart, I was thinking, *why should I say "sorry" to them? It is they who wronged me!* Nevertheless, I went to my room and knelt down to pray, and the Lord spoke. He said, "Shan, you need to apologise to your parents." "But why?" I complained. The Lord answered, "Because you have been punishing your parents by deliberately distancing yourself from them, knowing that'll get to them because they care about you." I was dumbstruck. I realised what the Lord said was true. I did not know I was unconsciously doing that out of hurt and resentment. I felt convicted. I knew apologising to my parents would be the right thing to do, no matter how hard it was.

The next morning, I went to my parents' hotel room and said to them, "Mum, dad, I'm sorry." All three of us wept. Mum said to me, "Shan, I love you. Had I known the way I loved you also hurt you, and if time could go back, I wouldn't have done it the same way." It was the first time I heard mum say, "I love you", and it was the first time she acknowledged how I was treated was wrong. It meant the world to me. It felt like the beginning of healing.

The Sanctification in The Family

My family and I come from a reserved culture where the phrase "I love you" is not commonly used, not even between parents and children. Instead, people are more used to expressing love through what they do for others. However, I have since learnt that language is so powerful. God spoke the world into being. His Son is called Logos, the Word of God. There is something about the verbal expression of love that cannot be replaced by anything else. Of course, it can become blasé in everyday use. But "I love you", when said and genuinely meant by a person, makes known the person's heart towards another person unambiguously, and that can mean so much...

That day was the last day of mum and dad's visit. We cried all the way on the train to London Heathrow.

I wish I could tell you that was it, but that was only a prelude. Cutting the umbilical cord needs to set us apart spiritually from our blood family and

The Sanctification in The Family

result in a fundamental change in what we are made of, i.e., being rid of certain key features of the sinful nature passed down in the family and instead, taking on God's divine nature – the so-called 'renewal'. For me, this did not take place until eight years later. My explanation would be that the Father had to wait till I had developed sufficient intimacy with the Son so that I would have the incentive and will to persevere through this part of sanctification. This is because, from experience, the 'surgical removal' of the fleshly umbilical cord involved considerable agony. The Father is gentle and knows our limits [1]. In a season when I had to move back in with my parents temporarily, the process began.

I could not run away this time, nor did I want to. I understand for some of us how hard it can be to spend time with our parents. They seem to know where all our buttons are, and they press them every time (this is often, though not always, to do with unhealed family wounds in our souls). Trust

The Sanctification in The Family

me; I have been there... So, to avoid annoyance, irritation, anger, or hurt, we run, push them away, and shut them out of our lives. Sadly, I have been there too... However, this could hurt our parents, who, despite not being able to be the kind of father and mother we have hoped them to be, could nonetheless love us. Except in some cases where, unfortunately, associating with a parent(s) indeed puts us in harm's way or where the Lord Himself, for whatever reason, instructs us to take some time off from our parents, I have discovered from my experience that there are benefits in being in close proximity when it comes to the sanctification in the family.

Firstly, we tend to be most real when we are with our parents, who have known us since birth. We do not bother to put on façades like we often unconsciously do before others to hide our problems and weaknesses. When we are in such a state, God can get straight in there to work on our 'real self', whereas, at other times, He has to

The Sanctification in The Family

dismantle our disguise first, which is an extra step and takes time. Generally speaking, we grow quicker in God when we are real. Jesus taught us, *"When you pray, go into your room and shut the door and pray to your Father who is in secret. And your Father who sees in secret will reward you"* [2]. Most of my personal overcoming takes place in the secret place where I can be extremely real with God and myself.

Secondly, since our bodies come from our fathers and mothers, our flesh is almost identical to theirs with mirroring 'patches', i.e., the same areas of sinful nature. Therefore, our parents can serve as a mirror in which we can see what our old self, born of flesh and blood, is like – its ugliness. When I was shown that the blemishes I saw in my parents and was annoyed with, I actually had them too, the weaknesses I saw in them and despised, I had them too, and the way they sinned against me and hurt me, I did it to them and others too, it was very humbling. I lost confidence in my flesh. In fact, I earnestly begged God to help circumcise it because I did not want to carry those things in me or pass them on to my descendants – some incentives for sanctification! [3]

Thirdly, close interactions with our parents can help us recognise the critical areas in which our heavenly Father wishes to re-father and re-mother us. Family wounds can feel like hurt, self-pity, anger, resentment, etc., tangled in one big emotional mess. You are not feeling good, but you cannot quite tell what is what. However, the Father wants to untangle it all for us. He wants to pinpoint issues, events, and patterns of behaviour that have contributed to our way of being today to bring redemption and healing to each area. Though painful at times, my interactions with my parents led to revelations about why I was the way I was and how the Father wanted me to be.

Now, the overcoming. Firstly, the principle.

The Sanctification in The Family

As with the general principle and mechanism of sanctification stated in the last chapter, it is by obeying God's righteousness, i.e., doing what is right in God's eyes as expressed in His words, that we crucify the old self with its sinful nature. And in the case of the sanctification in the family, it is loving, honouring, and obeying our fathers and mothers in the Lord, according to the below righteous commands of God:

Honour your father and mother, and you shall love your neighbour as yourself. (Mat 19:19)

Children, obey your parents IN THE LORD, *for this is right.* ***"Honour your father and mother"*** *(this is the first commandment with a promise), "that it may go well with you and that you may live long in the land."* (Eph 6:1-3; Exo 20:12; Deu 5:16)

Children, obey your parents in everything, *for this pleases the Lord.* (Col 3:20)

The Sanctification in The Family

The principle of sanctification is the same for everyone. Still, the process will look different for each person because we have different fathers and mothers, different flesh, different experiences of upbringing and childhood events, different family situations, and possibly are at different life stages. There is no one-size-fits-all formula. Each person can only follow the Father's leading through the Holy Spirit for a process precisely tailored to him. That is why I will not share what this process looked like for me personally. Still, only crucial takeaways from it, along with some of the revelations received. I hope that some of them, if not all, can facilitate others' overcoming in their families. Here they are.

1. We do not wrestle against flesh and blood [4]. Our parents are not our enemies; the demonic spirits behind their flesh are.

A 'patch' of flesh/an area of sinful nature of any person, when uncrucified, is like a lever that an evil

The Sanctification in The Family

spirit can use to incite the person to sin against God or/and others (hence why sanctification is important; it shuts the doors). Sometimes, when someone attacks me, I can sense the demonic presence behind them. So, when parents sin against us, *they know not what they do* [5]. When the heart is lacerated, and the emotions are thrown into turmoil because of what a parent has said or done to us, **it is helpful to remind ourselves who our real enemy is**. Often, after being sinned against, we would start having thoughts of accusations against that parent and would even rehearse combative conversations in our head in which we always seemed to win the argument. These thoughts are not necessarily our own but are often the voices of the accuser [6]. This is the warfare dimension of overcoming the flesh.

See, this is the game the devil plays: he first incites your father/mother to sin against you, and then he plants thoughts of accusations in your mind against him/her. If we keep entertaining those thoughts, we will trap ourselves in endless bitterness and judgement against that parent and would be gratifying our flesh rather than crucifying it. However, if we keep resisting those thoughts and refusing to yield to the lust of the flesh to take the Judge's seat, sooner or later, the devil will flee from us [7]. We are to *take every thought captive to obey Christ* [8]. In wrestling against the enemy, I find it effective to speak out loud and command the evil spirit to shut up and be gone.

2. It is beneficial to hold the tongue and not speak back or defend ourselves.

The Bible says that *"the tongue is a fire, a world of unrighteousness"*, *"a restless evil, full of deadly poison"*[9], and it encourages us not to *"repay evil for evil or reviling for reviling"*, but to *"overcome evil with good"*[10]. A massive amount of dishonouring is done through the tongue. Whether a parent is in the wrong or not, there is no benefit in antagonising him/her, and neither is it our responsibility or place to educate a parent on how to be a father/mother to us; it is not right that we try to 'father/mother' them instead. It may be true that we know more about God than our parents, who are not yet saved or not as mature spiritually. However, force-explaining spiritual truths to their natural self would be in vain, for the Word says, *"The natural person does not accept the things of the Spirit of God, for they are folly to him, and he is not able to understand them because they are spiritually discerned"*[11]. Bringing God into our defence would only agitate a parent even more. If the parent is not saved yet, it will reflect badly on Christianity, which they may blame for the child's 'rebellion'. If the parent is saved, weaponising the Word of God only for it to be used as a double-edged sword against a believing parent can be very damaging [12].

Think about Jesus. *He was oppressed, and He was afflicted, yet **He opened not his mouth**; like a lamb that is led to the slaughter, and **like a sheep that*** *before its shearers is silent, so He opened not his mouth* [13]. ***When He was reviled, He did not revile in return;*** *when He suffered, He did not threaten, but continued entrusting Himself to the Father who judges justly* [14]. Jesus knew that the people's hearts were dull, their eyes could not see, and their ears could not hear [15]; they would not have understood even if He explained why He had to endure the Cross for their sake. Besides, trying to preserve Himself through defence would contradict the purpose for which He came – to die as a ransom for humankind [16]. It is the same for us today.

Our goal is to PUT TO DEATH OUR OLD SELF, not to preserve it through self defence. Our intentionally resisting the lust of the flesh, not taking the matter of justice into our own hands, and patiently enduring the 'verbal scourging' would unite us with Christ IN A DEATH LIKE HIS so that we may also be united with Him IN A RESURRECTION LIKE HIS [17]. Nevertheless, let us not suffer for misbehaving. For what credit is it if, when we sin and are beaten for it, we endure? [18] Our fathers and mothers have the authority given by God to discipline us [19].

3. As a 'patch' of flesh/an area of sinful nature in a parent is highlighted, it is good to ask the Father what He is like in that area in contrast to that parent and forgive.

Truth can be painful, but it can set us free [20]. Indeed, we are commanded by God to love and forgive, but mercy is not denying the truth. We need to clearly define how a parent has sinned against us in a specific area, i.e., how exactly have they fallen short of the heavenly Father, instead of just forgiving in general, vague terms. I remember when I learnt what the Father is like compared with a parent in a particular area; on the one hand, I was greatly grieved by the truth that I had not been treated right in that area all my life; on the other hand, I felt comforted by the knowledge that the

Father has got me and is now making it right. Such a mix of deep emotions made Psalm 27:10 especially real: *"For my father and my mother have forsaken me, but the Lord will take me in."* **In this way, I came to know the Father more and more intimately and began to be re-fathered and re-mothered by Him in particular areas.**

Moreover, once my eyes are opened to see the truth, including the Father's standard in an area, I often would realise that I fall short of that standard and have also committed the same sin against others in the past as a parent has against me. Of course, I carry the same flesh! Jesus said, *"First take the log out of your own eye, and then you will see clearly"*[21]. **This brings humility and a heart change, which leads to repentance.** As I repent and ask the Father for forgiveness for my sin, I also forgive that parent of the same sin. Jesus said, *"If you forgive others their trespasses, your heavenly Father will also forgive you, but if you do not forgive others their* *trespasses, neither will your Father forgive your trespasses"* [22]. Truth is not without mercy.

Forgiveness is an inseparable part of loving our fathers and mothers, which falls under the second greatest commandment, 'love your neighbour as yourself' [23]. It is instrumental in bringing about healing. Some of us struggle with unforgiveness, and one of the common reasons is that we want to wait till we feel like forgiving. This is effectively waiting for our flesh to give us strength so we can feel ready to forgive. The problem is, it never will! There is nothing good in our flesh [24]. The flesh is opposed to the Spirit and cannot submit to God's law [25]; plus, why would it give us power so that we can kill it? It is by intentionally choosing to forgive in obedience to God's righteous command and by the empowerment of the Spirit that we kill it.

By grace, the Lord always puts us in the most favourable position to choose to obey His righteous command over the lust of our flesh, but we still have to make that decision. **Forgiveness is a CHOICE. We decide to forgive our fathers and mothers regardless of what they have said or done to us, and God will supply more grace to bring forgiveness to completion.** We may not feel able to let go of resentment overnight or pass the test in one go, but God is merciful and patient, and He sympathises with our weaknesses (hence no need to self-condemn). We can always repent and try again. As long as we persevere and are determined to forgive no matter what, eventually, it will be done!

4. It would be helpful to find out what made our fathers and mothers the persons they are, specifically, what their parents were like towards them when they were growing up.

Yielding to the same 'patches' of flesh or the same areas of sinful nature passed down in the family, it is likely that in the same places and same ways our parents have sinned against us, our grandparents have sinned against them. **Knowing about our parents' upbringing can help us identify the generational strongholds or repeating patterns of sins in the family.**

Personally, I invited my parents to share their childhood, as it was okay for me to do so. I then saw clearly that they have been victims of their fathers' and mothers' brokenness and that it is only **by grace** that I have been taken further to see the spiritual dynamics at work and been given the tools to overcome, whereas they have not. I would not know what I would have been like if I were left in their shoes. When I began to see at that level, I was filled with gratitude towards God and **compassion towards my father and mother**, making forgiving easier. The good news is that our overcoming in the family means our children and our children's children would no longer have to be subject to the same generational strongholds. It stops here, at our generation.

5. Ask the Father to enable us to love our parents and heal us.

Forgiving and being healed are two different things; forgiving does not always automatically lead to healing. In my experience, sometimes there was a gap period, during which I did not resent a parent in the area I was sinned against anymore, but I did not yet feel I could love that parent. This may be explained as such: Although a 'patch' of flesh/an area of sinful nature has been crucified (hence we cannot sin in that area anymore, unless wilfully), creating a vacuum, the person has not yet been resurrected in that area, i.e., his spirit man has not yet grown into a new measure of the image and stature of Christ to fill that vacuum [26]; just like there were three days before Jesus was raised from the dead. **But *ask, and it will be given to you*[27].**

It might be different for you, as for me, when the moment of resurrection comes, often I would feel a gentle warmth flooding my being as if I am being

The Sanctification in The Family

salved with the balm of heaven that releases healing to my soul. It is an amazing, powerful, emotional experience! As a new measure of Christ, who is the image of God, who is love, is formed in me [28], I would be filled with a new love for that parent, such that their wrong in that area is covered under this new measure of love and therefore no longer bothers me [29]. **Eventually, after overcoming in one area after another, we would have so much of God's perfect love formed in us that we would be able to overlook all our parents' sins and blemishes and love them just as they are. They have not changed; we have been transformed and sanctified.**

6. We may need to reassure our parents that we love them.

Although seemingly most of the activities happen on our side, our parents can nonetheless feel the pain when the umbilical cord is being cut. After all, an umbilical cord has two ends. When the spiritual detachment takes place, they may no longer feel 'in sync' with us, i.e., can no longer understand our ways, thoughts, choices, etc., having done so since we were born. Consequently, they might panic, feeling as if they were losing us. This is regardless of whether they are believers or not. I can imagine that most parents would find it really hard, and some might react if controlling others has been an issue. If this happens, we should be mindful of what our parents are experiencing and reassure them that we love them and will always be their children through words, body language, or any other love language that speaks to them. Soon, they will realise that we love them more than before, with a much purer love. In my case, cutting the umbilical cord has led to **a godlier, more love-filled, closer relationship with my father and mother.**

A child is a gift from God and is 'loaned' to a father and mother to be brought up in the discipline and instruction of the Lord [30]. However, due to a father and mother's imperfection, inevitably, they fall short of how the Father Himself would have parented. From a father and mother's perspective, allowing a child to cut off the umbilical cord is effectively handing the child back to God, from whom the child came, and who loves the child even more than they do, both to right the wrongs and to take the child further and higher than they themselves are ever able to. Because Hannah did not cling to Samuel and was willing to hand him back to God, the boy had a chance to go on to become one of the greatest prophets of Israel [31]. Understandably, letting go of someone into whom one has poured so much throughout one's parenthood is hard, especially for a mother to whom the umbilical cord directly connects; it takes **deep selfless love**... On the other hand, from a child's perspective, even when we find ourselves in a situation where our father or/and mother are unwilling to let go, we still have to do it; **the responsibility of cutting the umbilical cord lies with us**. Jesus said, "*Whoever loves father or* *mother more than Me is not worthy of Me..."* [32]. The truth is that only as we learn to love God, which is obeying His words and doing His will [33], are we truly able to love those around us with God's perfect love. Have we not all been initiated into the royal priesthood? [34] Being set apart from our blood families is an essential step towards living a life totally consecrated onto God.

7. It is necessary to set boundaries with wisdom and discernment from God.

Even though key mirroring 'patches' of flesh on our side have been crucified, they are not yet so on our parents' side. Hence, it is still possible that the enemy may attempt to sway us via their flesh to make us move outside the will of God because he is an opportunist and knows that God commands us to obey our fathers and mothers. So, there is a need to set boundaries. However, this does not mean trying to be our own protector pushing our parents away, or muzzling them. **The boundaries**

are to be drawn with the help of the Lord, with the sense of assurance that He is our ultimate Covering; no harm shall befall us even when our parents fail to cover us from the enemy's attack; no one can derail us from the path God sets out for us even when our parents out of their brokenness misguide us; no one can snatch us out of the Father's hand [35].

Setting boundaries involves a considerable understanding of our fathers' and mothers' authority. God delegates our parents' authority over us for our good, so essentially obeying them is obeying God's authority, and rebelling against them is rebelling against God's authority. However, this looks differently at different stages of our personal development. We needed our parents' discipline and instructions when we were children because our physical and mental capacities were still developing. Galatians 4:1-2 says that "*a child is no different from a slave*...he is under guardians and managers until **the date** set by his *father*". 'The date', in terms of personal development, in my opinion, has several levels of meaning. In the natural sense, it refers to reaching adulthood, where we become capable of forming our own judgements and making decisions for ourselves in life. In the spiritual sense, it represents: firstly, being set free from 'the elementary principles of the world' and receiving the Spirit of adoption into our hearts whereby we become born-again, as Galatians 4:3-7 goes on to say; and secondly, reaching a place of spiritual maturity where we become intimately acquainted with the Father and His will for our lives, and live the rest of our lives according to His will, which, I believe, is the highest destiny a person can have and yields the greatest eternal reward. Ideally, parents can accurately discern the different stages of personal development we are at and adjust accordingly while exercising their authority. However, due to their limitations, from experience, we know this is not always the case, and conflicts can arise at times as a result. In the West, where

The Sanctification in The Family

the notion of personal freedom is widely embraced, this may be less of an issue once a person becomes an adult. However, for those who come from cultures where parents continue to exercise authority in a paternalistic manner in their children's lives even when they are adults, the tension can be very real, particularly if the child wants to act according to God's will. Still, the parents themselves are not walking closely with God. Obey or disobey, where is the line?

Whilst we are commanded by God to obey our fathers and mothers, we are to do so IN THE LORD[36]. In other words, we are not required to obey if a parent's instruction contradicts the logos (written) or rhema (inspired) word of God, given we have discerned correctly with a clear conscience. Jesus said, *"If you love Me, you will keep My commandments* [37]*"*, and He also said, *"Whoever loves father or mother more than Me is not worthy of me* [38]*"*. This effectively suggests that we cannot obey our earthly fathers or mothers more than we obey God, no matter how our parents take it, what the cultural setting is (for kingdom culture is higher than human culture), or what other people say around you. Though we may face chastisement or even persecution, God has to come first [39].

The instruction of the Lord is the solid rock we can stand on and the final authority against which all attempts to challenge shall falter [40].

Over time, you will discover that obeying God is the only way to victory and ensure our continued access to God's favour and protection.

Nevertheless, a parent's instruction may be indeed from God; it is just that we do not like it. Cutting the umbilical cord does not mean our fathers and mothers cease to serve the God-mandated purpose of instructing their children or cease to have authority over their children. God can still speak through them, even when they are non-Christians, because God creates all families, and the orders therein are ordained by Him [41]. Whereas in the past, we held judgement against our parents and did not have the ears to hear what God might be saying through them and therefore might have acted foolishly in rebellion, our overcoming in the family should bring new humility and softening of heart, such that we are willing to pay attention to our parents' voice and try to discern God's voice in its midst.

The key is not to lean on our own understanding but ask the Lord to help us **discern case by case** whether a thing a parent has asked of us is from God or not, and ask Him to give us wisdom on what we ought or ought not to do in each case; and if it is from the enemy, how we can resist the demonic spirit behind while keeping loving that parent [42]. **In doing so, gradually, the boundary lines are dotted and drawn. These boundaries carry spiritual authority because they have been drawn based on God's instructions.**

The Sanctification in The Family

There are two contrasting examples in the Bible: Deceit is never right, but because Jacob obeyed his mother Rebekah, to whom the Lord had foretold that *"the older shall serve the younger"*, and did as she asked, he was able to inherit the blessing from his father Isaac [43]. Solomon honoured his mother, Bathsheba, who saved his life and throne. When she came to see him, he rose to meet her, bowed down to her, and had a seat brought for her to sit on his right, and he promised to grant her request. However, when his mother asked for Abishag to be given to Adonijah, who had previously usurped the throne and had sneakily exploited Bathsheba's weakness, Solomon sensed the treachery behind it. Hence, he could not obey; instead, he put Adonijah to death[44]. As you can see, it is not straightforward, but the Holy Spirit will teach and show us what to do in each situation.

Practising deciphering over and over again what the source and nature of our parents' instructions are, helps to train our 'powers of discernment' [45], which would benefit our Christian walk hugely. It enables us to discern what is truth and what is the will of God, unswayed by the opinions of men [46]. This, then, allows us always to follow the Headship of Christ and grow in wisdom to know what to do in situations where instructions from human authority contradict God's. (The Headship of Christ is expounded in *Last Eve*, the first book of the *Mystery of Sanctification* series.)

8. The purpose of cutting the fleshly umbilical cord is so that we would enter into an intimate relationship with the Father and live a life in abandonment to Him.

Personally, cutting the fleshly umbilical cord marks a watershed in my Christian journey. It is like I have been 'claimed' by the Father and made free to follow His leading, learn His ways, do His will, and live according to His plans without being held back by the family, and this has accelerated my spiritual growth. My heart in sharing the above is to encourage others to find their own journeys of overcoming in the family, become intimately acquainted with the Father themselves, and so begin to live a life in abandonment to Him. While what I shared may be of help – by God's grace, my experience cannot be replicated, as **the journey of the sanctification in the family is individually tailored.** Only the Father has the full knowledge of what and how, and when, and He conveys such to us by His Spirit through scriptures, dreams, visions, pictures, words of knowledge, and other forms of rhema word. Only He has the power to make it happen. We should follow His leading step by step throughout this process faithfully.

It is by intimately journeying and communing with the Father in this reasonably deep part of sanctification, in which we fully open ourselves to Him, all our pains and struggles, and let Him help us untangle them all and redeem the past, that we get to know what the Father is really like and find healing, freedom, love, and acceptance in Him.

The Sanctification in The Family

1. (1Co 10:13) **2.** (Mat 6:6) **3.** (Col 2:11) **4.** (Eph 6:12) **5.** (Luk 23:34) **6.** (Zec 3:1; Rev 12:10) **7.** (Jas 4:7,12) **8.** (2Co 10:5) **9.** (Jas 3:6,8) **10.** (1Pe 3:9; Rom 12:17,21) **11.** (1Co 2:14) **12.** (Heb 4:12; Eph 6:17) **13.** (Isa 53:7) **14.** (1Pe 2:23) **15.** (Mat 13:15) **16.** (Joh 12:27) **17.** (Rom 6:5,8) **18.** (1Pe 2:20; 3:17; 4:15) **19.** (Rom 13:1; Eph 6:4) **20.** (Joh 8:32) **21.** (Mat 7:5) **22.** (Mat 6:14-15) **23.** (Mat 22:37-39) **24.** (Rom 7:18) **25.** (Gal 5:17; Rom 8:7) **26.** (Rom 6:4-8) **27.** (Mat 7:7) **28.** (1Jn 4:8,16; Gal 4:19) **29.** (1Pe 4:8) **30.** (Eph 6:4) **31.** (1Sa 1-2; 3:19) **32.** (Mat 10:37) **33.** (Joh 14:21-24) **34.** (1Pe 2:9) **35.** (Joh 10:29) **36.** (Eph 6:1) **37.** (Joh 14:15) **38.** (Mat 10:37) **39.** (Act 5:29) **40.** (Mat 7:24-25) **41.** (Eph 3:14-15) **42.** (Pro 3:5-6) **43.** (Gen 25:23; 27:8-17) **44.** (1Ki 1:11-21,28-31; 2:13-25) **45.** (Heb 5:14) **46.** (Rom 12:2; Mar 12:14; Gal 2:6; Eph 4:14)

iv. From Brokenness to Wholeness

Sanctification is the will of God for us [1]. God desires that we would make the right choice at each crossroads, that is, choose to obey His righteous command rather than our own flesh in every life circumstance orchestrated and presented by the Spirit, and thus continually advance in sanctification. However, from my experience in ministry and general observation, the church's teachings predominantly focus on 'justification by faith'; there has been a lack of emphasis on the need for sanctification and an explanation of how it works. As a result, many believers are unaware of the role they ought to play in their sanctification, namely obeying God's words, and therefore have not been able to *leave the elementary doctrine of Christ and go on to maturity* [2]. Some churches and people groups are hungry for more. Yet their hunger often is directed towards the pursuit of knowledge, revelations, the gifts of the Spirit, the manifest presence of God, signs, wonders, and

The Sanctification in The Family

miracles, rather than obedience to God's words, without which there can be no true spiritual advancement. Then, there is also the version of teaching on the grace that more excuses disobedience than empowers believers to obey God's righteousness, contributing to a generally casual attitude towards sin and hardness of heart. When it comes to the sanctification in the family, the above factors can all come into play, plus shying away from tackling family wounds because of the pain involved.

I appreciate that unearthing deep childhood wounds can be excruciating. I know because I went through it. But I also know that if I did not allow the Father to take my hands and take me back to where the damage was done to walk me through those areas and events, and if I did not choose to love, honour and obey my father and mother in the Lord in obedience to God's righteous commands, and, in doing so, crucify the sinful flesh, my spirit man would not have been able to grow into a new measure of the image of the Father in Christ, nor could my soul receive healing. I would have stayed as a broken individual, a needy orphan at heart, always unconsciously using and hurting the people around me, and never truly able to experience the freedom of the newness of life as a son, regardless of what I profess, what I know theologically, what prophetic promises I have received, what gifts I have, what I do for God, and so on.

One of my great passions is to see believers released into their destinies and callings, and it always pains my heart to see someone being held back by brokenness, despite having an extremely high level of gifting. It, too, concerns me when I see individuals minister out of brokenness; it becomes about them, which often leads to control and manipulation, and it also taints the gifting, which can cause more damage than build others up...

The Sanctification in The Family

Oh, how overcoming in the family is desperately needed to transform this orphan generation from brokenness to wholeness!

In almost all cases, brokenness can be traced back to one's relationship with his father and mother. As mentioned in the last chapter, our 'self' is made of identical, mirroring 'patches' of flesh as our parents. This means whenever we despise our fathers and mothers, we effectively despise ourselves, and often we struggle with insecurity and low self-esteem. Whenever we reject our fathers and mothers, we effectively reject ourselves, and often we would be subject to self-rejection and sometimes even self-harm. Whenever we judge our fathers and mothers effectively, we pass judgement on ourselves, and therefore we would suffer self-condemnation. We cannot have two kinds of measures; the measures we use against our fathers and mothers would be the same ones we use against ourselves [3]. The issues that we commonly struggle with are rooted in the family. This is because **our well-being and spiritual soundness are directly tied to the condition of our hearts toward our fathers and mothers**.

I am far from being sorted, but the reconciliation with my father and mother in the heart has brought me tremendous peace, for such ultimately is reconciliation with my 'self'. I am now at peace with my 'self', accepting who I am and where I am in my journey. I can finally just 'be'; poised and cocooned in the Father's acceptance and love, wherever I am. This is such a good feeling! I really hope everyone can taste it and see it for themselves!

While the sanctification in the family through reconciling with our fathers and mothers in the heart (with God's help) is possible regardless of one's parental status, it is generally more convenient when one's father and mother are still alive and more glorious if reconciliation can also be reflected in the natural. I have seen cases where the Lord graciously prolongs a parent's life for the sake of a believer so that they have enough time to accomplish this. So, if you still have an opportunity today, please do not wait.

In addition, God painted a mega illustration in the Old Testament to help us understand our spiritual journey in Christ, explicitly speaking: the land of Canaan is a type of the true Promised Land – God Himself; the Israelites' journey from being set free from slavery in Egypt to fully possessing the land of Canaan symbolises our spiritual journey from being born again to fully partaking in God's divine nature [4] – the journey of sanctification. Ephesians 6:1-3 says, *"Children, obey your parents in the Lord, for this is right. 'Honour your father and mother' (this is the first commandment with **A PROMISE**), '**that it may GO WELL WITH YOU and that you may LIVE LONG IN THE LAND**'."* This exhortation reaffirms the commandment in the Old Testament:

"Honour your father and your mother, that your days may be long in the land that the LORD your God is giving you." (Exodus 20:12)

"Honour your father and your mother, as the Lord your God commanded you, that your days may be long, and that it may go well with you in the land that the Lord your God is giving you." (Deuteronomy 5:16)

The Lord, by His will, has associated honouring fathers and mothers with one's fortune in the Promised Land. **Under the New Covenant, this means God promises us that if we obey His command to honour our fathers and mothers, we will be able to enjoy His grace and favour ('go well with you') and continually abide in Him ('live long in the land', which represents God Himself).** Certainly, in my personal life, I have noticed that whenever I am not loving my parents well, there would be a disruption to my communion with God, the presence would lift, and the grace would dry up, even for the works I am doing for God, such that I have to make it right first to get back on track. Conversely, whenever I love my parents well, I swim in God's presence and grace, filled with peace and joy, and everything I do tends to go so smoothly and efficiently.

1. (1Th 4:3) **2.** (Heb 6:1-2) **3.** (Mat 7:2; Deu 25:13-16, NASB) **4.** (2Pe 1:3-4)

v. The Masculine and Feminine Traits of God

You may have noticed that I have been using the terms 'being fathered/re-fathered' AND 'being mothered/re-mothered' by God. This is because I have discovered that another wonderful fruit of sanctification in the family is the restoration and rebalancing of God's masculine and feminine traits in us.

Although known as 'the Father', God is Spirit [1], He is neither male nor female as we understand in human terms, yet He has both masculine characteristics, such as defender, passion for justice, reasoning, decision-making, problem-solving and initiative, and feminine characteristics, such as empathy, compassion, intuition, and the ability to comfort and nurture. **Since He has both masculine and feminine traits, God is, in fact, both 'Father' and 'Mother' to us.** [a]

The Sanctification in The Family

We see in the Bible, in one place, it says that God is *"A father of the fatherless, and a judge for the widows"* [2]; in another place, it says, *"Can a woman forget her nursing child, that she should have no compassion on the son of her womb? Even these may forget, yet I will not forget you."* [3] In one place, it says, *"You, O LORD, are our Father, our Redeemer from of old is Your name"* [4]; in another place it says, *"As one whom his mother comforts, so I will comfort you; you shall be comforted in Jerusalem"*[5], and again, *"O Jerusalem, Jerusalem, the city that kills the prophets and stones those who are sent to it! How often would I have gathered your children together as a hen gathers her brood under her wings, and you were not willing!"* [6].

The Christian book and the same-titled film 'The Shack' captured this revelation very well. [b] The main character Mackenzie suffered physical and emotional abuse as a child at the hands of his violently alcoholic father. Hence to him, the image of 'father' is totally marred. For him to be able to

THE ROAD TO FULFILMENT | 125

relate, God appears to him as a mother figure to take him through healing, which includes reconciliation with his late father. However, towards the end of the story, before showing Mack where his missing daughter Missy's body is, God appears to him as a father figure, knowing for what they are about to do, Mack would need a father by his side.

When God created 'Man' in His own image after His own likeness [7], this 'Man' was created to embody God's masculinity and femininity. When God took the woman out of 'Man', He assigned a greater degree of feminine traits to her, leaving a greater degree of masculine traits with the man [8]. When the man and the woman became one in marriage, they became 'Man' again [9], fully embodying God's masculine and feminine traits, both of which make up His perfect image. [c] **Therefore, the oneness of a husband and wife in marriage reflects the complete image of God.** Additionally, a dear brother helped me understand that, parallel to the

The Sanctification in The Family

picture of a marriage where positionally the husband is the head and covering of the wife [10], although God's image encompasses masculine and feminine traits, His femininity is covered under His masculinity. That is why He will always be known as 'the Father', never 'the Mother', yet He is both.

It is observable that, to varying degrees and proportions, all image-bearers of God still carry both the masculine and feminine traits of God despite the Fall. **However, falling short of the glory of God means that a person no longer bears a trait of God to the perfect degree and that the optimal allocation of God's masculine and feminine traits in men and women has also been distorted.** For example, men can suffer the impairment of masculinity. When God questioned Adam if he had eaten of the tree of which He had commanded him not to eat, he did not quite 'be a man' to take full responsibility for the Fall as the head of the marriage. Instead, he blamed it on Eve, saying, *"The woman whom you gave to be with me,* *she gave me fruit of the tree, and I ate"* [11]. He withdrew his covering from his wife and was prepared to let the wrath of God fall on her. Similarly, we see Abraham and Isaac were willing to put their wives' chastity and reputation at stake for their own safety and lied about their relationships [12]. We also see in Judges, a certain Levite made his concubine go out to be assaulted to death by the men of Gibeah who followed the cruel practice of Sodom and Gomorrah while he himself hid inside the house [13].

On the other hand, women can take on too much masculinity. For example, Jezebel was power-thirsty. As the wife of Ahab, the King of Israel, she usurped the headship in her marriage and became the de facto ruler of Israel. She incited her husband to do evil and killed the prophets of the Lord and installed 450 prophets of Baal and 400 prophets of Asherah who ate at her table [14], effectively keeping the whole nation under her control via pagan worship. After Ahab informed her that Elijah had

The Sanctification in The Family

killed all her prophets with the sword, she resorted to killing Elijah too [15]. She also used Ahab's name and seal to murder Naboth to covet his vineyard to get what her husband wanted while she could continue to rule through fear [16]. Jezebel's daughter Athaliah was also power-thirsty. She married Jehoram, the King of Judah, and corrupted her husband and son with her wicked counsel [17]. When she saw her son King Ahaziah was dead, she arose and destroyed all the legitimate successors except the infant Joash who Jehosheba secretly hid away. Athaliah then usurped the royal throne to rule as a queen regnant [18], and following her mother's wiles, she installed Baal worship over the kingdom of Judah [19].

It can be said that the predominant culture in society generally values masculine traits more than feminine traits. In the secular world, masculine traits such as reasoning, decision-making, initiative, and being driven are considered highly attractive. They are often associated with leadership qualities, whereas you would rarely find a job description that emphasises feminine traits such as empathy, compassion, intuition, and the ability to comfort and nurture, especially for management positions. This sways the general population toward people aspiring to acquire and demonstrate more masculine traits. As a former recruiter who has interviewed thousands of candidates, I regret to say that the above creates disadvantage and injustice not just for women but all who come from families where they are unable to receive sufficient input of masculine traits – not by their choice (explained later).

Whether compelled by life circumstances, peer pressure, or one's ambition, many women strive to put on more masculine traits to be on an equal playing field. But the standard itself was not equal to start with! Why do women have to change to become more like men? Why do women have to reject their femininity to become more masculine? Altogether, we find ourselves in a very masculine

The Sanctification in The Family

world shaped by powerful people with extreme masculine traits. We can keep things functioning but are primarily detached from our inner self, which arguably matters more to who we are as human beings.

Moreover, it can be said that the leaning toward masculinity is also present in the church. The type of governance commonly adopted by the church is similar to that of the corporations in the world, i.e., having different levels of ecclesiastical positions and governing through a chain of command. In contrast, the essential roles of marriage and family in the balanced upbuilding of the church arguably have been largely overlooked. The existing model historically allowed male clergy to take charge of ecclesiastical affairs independently, without or with minimal room for involvement for female believers. Having long missed the spiritual input of wives and mothers that should have come through the oneness in the marriages forged by husbands and wives genuinely, mutually laying down their lives

The Sanctification in The Family

for each other and under the safety of husbands' spiritual coverings, the church may be said to have overall taken a more masculine approach to theology.

The emphasis has been on, for instance, the wrath and judgement of God, the condemnation of sinners, the atonement of the Lamb, the requirement of religious discipline, etc., which are all fundamentally true and core, but if unbalanced by teachings that reflect God's feminine traits, can lead to a form of Christianity that is more about the intellectual understanding of theological concepts than the development of one's personal relationship with God. This does not do justice to a God who is, in fact, highly relational. Who sympathises with our weaknesses, who weeps with those who weep and comforts those who moan, who heals the broken-hearted and binds up their wounds, who knows us intimately and seeks to be intimately known by us, who loves communing with us daily, and who longs to dwell with us for

The Sanctification in The Family

eternity; these are wives and mothers' characteristics and specialties. Consequently, we make Him to be a very impersonal God that is limited to theology and religious formality, detached from believers' everyday walk.

In addition, this masculinity-oriented culture affects marriages in and outside the church. Within the traditional definition of marriage, like two magnets, men and women are supposed to be drawn to each other. Still, if we turn one of the magnets the other way, immediately, they would start repelling each other. If we ask an average guy, personality-wise, whether he prefers a 'man-like' woman or a 'woman-like' woman, I guess most guys would say the latter. Therefore, I think the above could be one of the significant factors contributing to the phenomenon of so many single women in modern society and that women who are very powerful according to worldly standards often find their love life unsatisfying.

The Sanctification in The Family

Since the beginning, there has been enmity between the serpent and women [20]. On the one hand, the ruler of the world orchestrates a masculine world such as this [21]; on the other hand, he lures us women into an unfair game to fight and compete with our fellow image-bearers. This is an invisible war waged by an invisible foe against women's femininity [d], to distort the beautiful image of God in them and to prevent them from fulfilling their God-given destiny – to be a picture of the glorious Church, the Bride of Christ [22], and a mother that imparts life to the nations! [23]

Regrettably, I once was a victim. I used to be emotionally shut down. Growing up, I learnt to suck it up and soldier on when experiencing tough times. The only way of life I knew and was good at was being competitive and performance-driven, which eventually landed me a job in the cut-throat, male-dominated investment banking world. After becoming a born-again Christian, I gradually learnt to tend to my internal feelings by processing things with the Lord. Finally, after being healed of much brokenness through the sanctification in the family, I felt as if a whole new world was opened up before my eyes.

As some feminine traits of God were restored in me, I became able to empathise with people and see from their eyes and feel their emotions, and I became more able to see from God's eyes and feel His heart for me and others. Both often make me weep, whether in a secret place or in front of others; I cannot help it. But at least I now know this is not a sign of weakness but of emotional health. This, in turn, has enabled me to be more sensitive to and perceive more accurately where people are at, to tend to their emotional needs, and comfort them with words of encouragement from God's heart when needed. The small victory in my personal life has made me realise what powerful gifts God has entrusted to us women if we would steward them well, beginning with restoring them in the family.

The Sanctification in The Family

Over time, I seem to notice that the impairment and disproportion of masculinity or femininity in a person often has to do with the abnormality in at least one of the parents, which makes obeying God's commands to love, honour and obey that parent in the Lord particularly important if one wishes to be restored and become what they are meant to be. The saying 'like father, like son; like mother, like daughter' is not entirely without reason. A son is intended to mainly inherit his masculine traits from his father at the right amount and, in the meantime, a healthy amount of feminine traits from his mother. Likewise, a daughter is meant to mainly inherit her feminine traits from her mother at the right amount, and in the meantime, a healthy amount of masculine traits from her father. However, because of the brokenness in our fathers and mothers, based on my own experience and observation, sometimes the below scenarios can occur:

The Sanctification in The Family

Scenario 1: If the father is super masculine, it is possible that a child may exhibit symptoms of 'masculinity surplus', being over-competitive, dominant, stubborn, obstinate, self-dependent, etc.; the so-called 'alpha male' or 'alpha female'. This can cause many relationship issues and is particularly problematic for a daughter who may constantly try to dominate other women and men.

Scenario 2: If the mother is very masculine (or absent), it is possible that a child may suffer a 'femininity deficit', being emotionally insensitive, lacking empathy, compassion, the ability to comfort and nurture, etc. This, again, can be particularly problematic for a daughter who takes on additional masculinity yet not enough femininity. Also, the kind of masculinity inherited from a mother cannot entirely replace or do the same job as the kind of masculinity inherited from a father, especially in extreme circumstances. Furthermore, being deprived of the comfort that comes from a feminine mother figure [24], a child may

The Sanctification in The Family

go on to seek comfort in other things and people, which can lead to unhealthy addictions, subtly or explicitly. [e] But God is our ultimate Comforter! [25] As one whom his mother comforts, so He will comfort all who are 'motherless' [26]

Scenario 3: If the father is very feminine (or absent), it is possible that a child may suffer a 'masculinity deficit', lacking confidence, decision-making, logic, problem-solving and organisational abilities, being passive, etc. This can be particularly problematic for a son whose manhood depends on the masculinity input from his father. Missing a masculine father figure, a child would typically be attracted to other masculine figures in life (male or female) in and outside the church, whom they perceive can give them a sense of security, direction, and structure and make decisions for them; this can even affect their spouse choice. As mentioned, this group comprises people the established masculine society deems weak, marginalises, and discriminates against. Since

The Sanctification in The Family

they are particularly vulnerable, God has great compassion for them, for He is a Father for the 'fatherless' [27].

If we compound **Scenario 2** with **Scenario 3**, we would then have a child who mainly inherits masculinity from a mother and femininity from a father, which, though still count as life skills, may fail to equip them fully for life situations where the proper kind of masculinity inherited from a father or femininity from a mother is needed.

Scenario 4: If the mother is super feminine, a child may exhibit symptoms of 'femininity surplus', being sentimental, overemotional, oversensitive, etc. This, again, can be particularly problematic for a son who is called to one day lead as the head of marriage and family.

The Sanctification in The Family

Subject Matter	with:	Masculinity	Femininity	Possible symptoms in a child	Solution: Love, honour and obey that parent in the Lord
Super masculine father	Relatively balanced mother	✓✓	✓	**Masculinity surplus:** overcompetitive, dominant, stubborn, self-willed, self-dependent	Erase surplus masculinity
Masculine (or absent) **mother**	Relatively balanced father	✓	✗	**Femininity deficit:** emotionally insensitive, lacking empathy, compassion, and the ability to comfort and nurture	Grow femininity
Feminine (or absent) **father**	Relatively balanced mother	✗	✓	**Masculinity deficit:** lacking confidence, logic, decision-making, problem-solving and organisational abilities, being passive	Grow masculinity
Super feminine mother	Relatively balanced father	✓	✓✓	**Femininity surplus:** sentimental, overemotional, oversensitive	Erase surplus femininity

I am aware that there are limitations to my experience and observation. Hence the four scenarios presented above may not be taken as conclusive or exhaustive (I imagine real-life situations are far more complex with varying degrees and combinations). However, they should suffice to help give some clues as to why we are the way we are and which parent we particularly need to love, honour and obey in the Lord and be reconciled with at heart. The truth is that no parent is perfect; compared with the heavenly Father Himself, all fathers and mothers have missed here or there. Therefore, it can be said that, to different extents, we have all been 'fatherless' and 'motherless'. But there is hope!

By being re-fathered and re-mothered by the heavenly Father, we can begin to learn what God is like as a perfect Father and a perfect Mother, and also tap into the original reservoir of God's masculinity and femininity to have our masculine and feminine traits increasingly repaired and reinstated to their optimal mix, so that a man can be a real man and a woman a real woman; and that the relationship between men and women may no longer be of competition, but of complement, leading to the forming of many 'Mans', all reflecting the glorious image of God.

1. (Joh 4:24) 2. (Psa 68:5, NASB) 3. (Isa 49:15) 4. (Isa 63:16) 5. (Isa 66:13) 6. (Mat 23:37) 7. (Gen 5:1-2) 8. (Gen 2:21-23) 9. (Gen 2:24) 10. (Eph 5:23; 1Co 11:3,10,15; Eze 16:8; Rut 3:9) 11. (Gen 3:11-12) 12. (Gen 12:11-20; 20:2-18; 26:6-11) 13. (Gen 19:4-9; Jdg 19:22-28) 14. (1Ki 18:4,19; 21:25) 15. (1Ki 19:1-2) 16. (1Ki 21:8-16) 17. (2Ki 8:18; 2Ch 22:2-3) 18. (2Ki 11:1-3) 19. (2Ch 24:7) 20. (Gen 3:15) 21. (1Jn 5:19) 22. (Eph 5:22-33) 23. (Gal 4:26-27; Isa 49:20-22; Eze 47:9) 24. (Psa 131:2) 25. (Joh 14:16) 26. (Isa 40:1; 66:13) 27. (Psa 68:5; 146:9; Deu 14:29; 24:19-21; Jas 1:27)

a. c. e. Denise Jordan. Session H: The Father Loves You (YouTube). (2006). Catch The Fire Toronto.
b. William P. Young. (2008). The Shack. Publisher: Hodder Windblown. ISBN: 9780340979495.
d. Denise Jordan. (2016). The War Against The Feminine (MP3). Fatherheart Ministries

vi. The Corporate Significance

Our collective overcoming of the orphan spirit, including our restoration of the masculine and feminine traits and their balance, can significantly improve the church's corporate life. It may be said that many of the issues we see in the body today can be traced back to the unhealed orphan hearts.

Like the older son in 'The Parable of the Prodigal Son,' who compares himself with his younger brother and is jealous and indignant about his father's gracious treatment of him, it can be said that a lot of the competition and infighting among believers ultimately boil down to the orphan hearts, that have not indeed known the Father's love and acceptance. Therefore, that compels us to strive for attention, affirmation, recognition, pre-eminence, and dominance, trying to get others to admire us, look up to us, and conform to our views, our ways, our choices, our passions, and callings… essentially taking the Father's place to 'father' and 'mother' others to make them **look like us**. However, when we are healed of our brokenness in the family, we would find such a sense of security and contentment in the Father that we cease looking elsewhere. Instead of trying to reproduce ourselves in other people out of our neediness, we would want to point them all to the Father, hoping they **become like Him**, and too find healing freedom and rest in Him, and walk into His plans for them.

Meanwhile, 'fatherlessness' tends to lead us to look up to the great men and women of God, even to the point of idolising them, habitually conforming to their views, their ways, their choices, their passions, and callings... essentially seeking to be 'fathered' and 'mothered' by them to **be like them**. But when our expectations are not met, or as soon as they say or do something that resembles our parents, our buttons would again be pressed, leading to more hurt, bitterness, and resentment. However, when we are healed of the orphan hearts

The Sanctification in The Family

and come to know the Father intimately, our deepest needs will be met in Him, and we will only aspire to **become like the Father** and who He has created us to be as individuals and only desire His will for our lives. Also, we would have more grace for those great men and women of God who are imperfect, just like us, covering their weaknesses and limitations with love, just like we do for our parents.

The above helps cultivate a healthy church environment where believers fellowship not out of neediness, nor is there pressure to perform, and where all members of the body are allowed to grow without ceilings and fulfil their respective functions as ordained by God. Might they be the apostles, prophets, evangelists, pastors, and teachers as the fivefold office and Christ's gifts to the body [1], or members of the body operating in various gifts of the Spirit, including the word of wisdom, word of knowledge, faith, gifts of healing, working of miracles, prophecy, discerning of spirits, tongues, interpretation of tongues, service, teaching, exhortation, generosity, leadership, acts of mercy, and helping and administrating [2]; rather than being stuck in **uniformity**, which is not true unity. (See *Last Eve* Chapter 6 'Fellowship in The Lord'. Christ's gifts and the gifts of the Spirit will be explained in another book of the *Mystery of Sanctification* series.)

---

1. (Eph 4:7-13) **2.** (1Co 12:4-11,28; 14:1-25; Rom 12:6-8; 1Pe 4:11)

vii. A Final Note

Today, I am grateful that I am filled with love for my father and mother, and as my heart is turned to them, the Father has also turned their hearts to me. Despite still having loose ends, I have already been able to reap so many blessings from what is now generally a healthy, godly relationship in line with God's order, from blocking the enemy's attacks to shielding me from inconvenient circumstances, from bringing God's correction to helping with my needs. Besides, having been healed of family wounds, my eyes have been opened to see the good traits I inherited from my father and mother, which makes me appreciate having them in my life even more. It once again proves that God's word is true and that our Father in heaven knows what is best for us if we simply believe and obey. Last but not least, with my parents' support and blessing, I have gained A BACKBONE and been released to charge forward toward my destiny and do everything God has called me to do. If my daddy and mummy are for me, I believe I can do all things! If all fails, they will still receive me and cover me as their child.

Here is the truth: Our earthly father and mother are God's blessing to our life, whether through the good things they have done for us or through their wrongs which allow us to become overcomers. They are part of our eternal testimony of overcoming; from before the foundation of the world, God already determined into which family we were to be born for our glory [1]. While the fellowship with brothers and sisters at church is precious, they cannot replace our father and mother's place. Our father and mother will be there when we are in dire need. If we are hit by a bus today, our father and mother will be among those who will come to collect our bodies and bury us. No matter how far we advance in the matters of the kingdom, we will still be our father and mother's child. No matter how far we travel in the world, we will still carry in our bodies their DNA. They will never cease to love us

The Sanctification in The Family

in the way they know and can, until they leave this world.

---

1. (Act 17:26)

IV.

The Treasures of All Nations

The healing of family wounds can help free us from all sorts of things that we, out of our neediness, occupy ourselves with and, therefore, afford us the ability to see beyond ourselves, such as spiritual issues pertaining to people groups. The final area I would like to discuss is **national identity**, which typically influences us without us knowing it. Without a correct relation to our national identity, we can be hindered from becoming who God has called us to be and fulfilling our God-given destinies as individuals and as people.

National identity, however, can be a sensitive topic. With all the geopolitical conflicts, age-old rivalries/grudges between nations, blocs, peoples, between the East and the West, the left and the right, and all the patriotism, nationalism, revisionism, etc., going on in the world, it is easy to step on a landmine and quickly arouse suspicion. However, I believe that there is a kingdom way of looking at it for us as Christians, which is above the ways of this world. I hope in what I am going to share; you will hear my heart and, more importantly, God's heart and be built up.

I have had a different Christian journey than many other believers in China. I was raised in Western Christianity, discipled by great men and women of God in the UK who are very deep and mature in the Lord and desire to see me grow into who God has called me to be. Meanwhile, I was profoundly impacted by a church in London that had a fivefold vision (i.e., the belief that all five offices of apostles, prophets, evangelists, pastors, and teachers are needed to bring the body of Christ to maturity based on Ephesians 4:11-13) and that frequently saw the manifest presence and glory of God come.

The Treasures of All Nations

It had a flat leadership team (or eldership) that shared platforms with congregation members with gifts and callings. Above all, the Lord Himself has been my teacher since I became saved, explaining scriptures to me and counselling me through all seasons of life, especially during those wilderness years when there was no Christian fellowship or guidance. I am grateful for my journey, and I am thankful to the Western church, which the Lord used to lay the foundation of my faith, to mould me as a believer and help me develop personal intimacy with Him, and to establish me firmly as a follower of Jesus Christ.

Admittedly, when the Lord first sent me back to work with the churches in China in a ministry capacity, there was a clash of church cultures. As a result, quite a few rough edges of mine were rubbed off... Nevertheless, by overcoming, through the Chinese churches, the Lord taught me the importance of honouring and submitting to God-appointed authority from the heart out of the fear of the Lord, of respecting and appreciating all who devote themselves to the ministry of the saints, of discipline, and of caring for fellow believers in word and deed – I was very touched that the believers in China looked after my needs while I was in their midst. I feel very blessed to glean from the Lord's churches both in the West and China, and I feel humbled to be used as an instrument to facilitate spiritual cross-pollination between the saints in these two parts of the world.

If I am to be compared to a lump of clay in the Potter's hand [1], then the Western church is where the Lord shaped me, and the Chinese church is where He trimmed me to give me a more refined look. However, no matter what this vessel will eventually become, its intrinsic characteristic and soul lie in the clay used in the beginning. For some of us to fulfil the purpose for which we were designed, we need to understand where we come from and reconnect with our roots. Here is my story.

The Treasures of All Nations

When I was a child, my mother bought me books of famous works by Western authors such as Jane Austen, Victor Hugo, Guy de Maupassant, and Gustave Flaubert. There began my fascination with the West. Never had I thought that one day I would have the opportunity to study and work in Britain and go on to become deeply acquainted with the culture and customs of this nation. For many years, from time to time, I pinched myself to see if I was really in this country which I only used to see in films when I was growing up. The carriages, the gentlemen in their morning dress, with a bit of smog half veiling the decorated buildings in the background, and a white Chinese subtitle at the bottom of the screen indicating the location: 伦敦 (London).

I met the Lord Jesus in London. I went to churches in London. When I had to move back to China in 2012, my heart broke. However, in retrospect, I can now see that more than church friends, what I was finding hard to let go of at that time was the lifestyle

The Treasures of All Nations

London or the nation of Britain afforded me. Nonetheless, I survived five years of the wilderness without any fellowship, leaning only on the Lord Himself, and eventually arrived at a place where I was so content with just being with the Lord that even if He were to leave me in China forever, I would still be fine. Then, out of nowhere, a job offer came from London! Wishing to be reunited with my church family, I accepted the offer and moved back to London. However, when the job was about to come through, the Lord said to me, "Shan, go back to China." By then, I had grown as a Christian and needed not the Lord to tell me twice; when He tells me something, I do it. This time, I did it without blinking an eye.

Britain was no longer my idol.

Around a year later, the Lord began to open up a new dimension of understanding of nations to me, starting with my own. One day, when I was praying and asking what to talk about in an introduction

The Treasures of All Nations

video for the *Mystery of Sanctification* book series, suddenly, the presence of God flooded the place where I was staying. There, I encountered the Lord and received a significant revelation about my nation, which has since evolved into one of my passions for God's people.

The Lord showed me that, in my subconscious, I had not assigned equal weight to the Chinese church as to the Western church, and that was due to **a hidden sense of inferiority** at the subconscious level as a Chinese national. The Lord then began to unveil to me how the events from the mid-19th century had impacted China spiritually and changed our people's **self-image**. I am no expert on history, but I will try to explain roughly what happened and its context.

China is one of the oldest civilisations on earth, with around 5,000 years of history. From the first unified dynasty, Qin (221BC), to the height of the last dynasty, Qing (end of 18th century), China was more or less the most powerful nation on earth. The former US Secretary of State Henry Kissinger put it this way: *"China... was never engaged in sustained contact with another country on the basis of equality for the simple reason that it never encountered societies of comparable culture or magnitude... In official Chinese records, foreign envoys did not come to the imperial court to engage in negotiations or affairs of state; they 'came to be transformed' by the Emperor's civilising influence. The Emperor did not hold 'summit meetings' with other heads of state; instead, audiences with him represented the 'tender cherishing of men from afar', who brought tribute to recognise his overlordship."* [a] However, this all changed when the Western nations developed swiftly through the Industrial Revolution, surpassing China in power, and the major event that shaped China today's state of being: The First Opium War (1839-1842). [b]

To counter the trade imbalance created by the demand for Chinese luxury goods, the British East

India Company smuggled opium into China and conducted the lucrative yet illegal sale of such. [c] Consequently, many Chinese became opium addicts, from which came the derogatory term 'the sick man of Asia', which still haunts many Chinese today. [d] The Qing government commissioned viceroy Lin Zexu to carry out a crackdown on the illegal opium trade. Lin initially attempted to get foreign merchants to forfeit their opium stores in exchange for tea, but it ultimately failed. So, he resorted to confiscation by force and destroyed a large quantity of opium. [e] In 1840, the British government responded by dispatching the Royal Navy, whose superior ships and guns the Chinese fleet could not withstand. [f] In 1842, China was forced to sign the 'Treaty of Nanking', which included ceding Hong Kong Island in perpetuity to Britain, opening five 'treaty ports' for trade, and paying Britain twenty-one million silver dollars. [g] This marked the beginning of a series of other invasions by Western powers and coerced signing of treaties of similar nature.

The Treasures of All Nations

Overnight, a noble prince became a pauper; imagine that kind of humiliation... The Western imperialism, together with the Japanese invasion, civil wars, political extremism, and utter poverty that China subsequently went through in the next 120 or so years, inflicted such a blow on the soul of the Chinese nation that we have never really recovered. (Just as a person's soul is affected by his life journey, the soul of a nation may be understood as the collective awareness of a people resulting from their shared history.) Blaming this on its own for being weak back then, China resolved to become strong via development so that it would never be bullied again by other nations. This was even written into our constitution.

However, though we build skyscrapers everywhere and host spectacular summits in an attempt to show the world that, today, as a people, we can stand on our own two feet; today, we are prosperous and powerful, yet beneath all that grandeur, still there is the broken soul; we care only too much how Westerners view us. Though the well-to-do among us today can afford luxury items, posh cars, and properties in the most expensive cities domestically and overseas or emigrate abroad altogether, with all that wealth, we are still not rid of the sense of inferiority as Chinese nationals. Still, sometimes we feel as if we are second-class people. This is because money can never be a remedy for the wounds in a soul. **As a nation, our soul has never been healed from the trauma of being forcibly subdued 180 years ago.**

I wept when I saw what my people had to carry and their helpless state. As I was kneeling there, sobbing, the Lord flooded me with His great love and compassion for China. I heard a cry from His heart similar to that of Matthew 23:37: *"O Jerusalem, Jerusalem... How often would I have gathered your children together as a hen gathers her brood under her wings..."*. I sensed the Lord standing there with His arms outstretched towards the Chinese sons and daughters, longing to cuddle

The Treasures of All Nations

us, heal us, and give us rest, a people who are afflicted, storm-tossed, not comforted, and heavy laden [2].

I then saw the Lord as a Potter moulding a lump of clay. I understood that lump of clay was me. I could feel His love towards the clay, and I heard Him say, "Shan, I did not make you a white person or of any other ethnicity; I made you a Chinese, having determined before the foundation of the world that you would be born into and raised up in a Chinese family. Shan, I love you, but I also love your people because with love, I made you; with love, I also made your people. Just as I watch over you, I also watch over them. Do you know, Shan, as a people, you have many qualities that delight Me, such as your hospitality, understanding of and submission to authority, and care for families and friends… But what delights me most is that once you receive Me as Lord, you have a great propensity to be wholehearted. You don't leave Me or forsake Me. You are zealous and walk with Me all the way to the

The Treasures of All Nations

end, regardless of what trials there might be. Also, as a people, you are very teachable, pliable, and willing to repent. Shan, do you know I have a great beautiful plan for China? I chose you, planted you, watered you, and now you are blossoming and beginning to bear fruit, but don't forget to share the first fruit with your own people. **You, yourself, have inherited the spiritual inheritance of the Chinese people.** Don't forget to serve your own people."

I was pierced to the heart when I heard these words of the Lord because I realised in the past, all I could see were the embarrassing stereotypical traits in my fellow countrymen. Over time, I developed contempt towards my people, such that I rejected my root (and hence, the sense of insecurity as a Chinese person), unable to see my people from the Lord's eyes. Feeling utterly convicted, I lay face down and wept bitterly. I repented and asked the Lord for forgiveness. There, I saw clearly that Christ Jesus is China's only hope: Only the Lord Jesus can heal us and deliver us as a people from the past trauma of suffering and humiliation.

Only as we see ourselves as the Lord sees, only in His love and His will and purpose for creating us, the Chinese people, in the very beginning, can we, as a people, stand tall with dignity. We have a place in this world simply because God created us. Only in Christ can we as a people find true identity, security, and purpose.

That was the beginning of an unfolding revelation. In the following weeks and months, the Lord started to show me the effect imperialism and colonialism can have on the people of a nation or territory and the body of Christ.

Once, through a friend, I met a man originally from Hong Kong, which used to be a British colony until its handover in 1997. In our brief conversation, he told me that he had long obtained British citizenship and that once he was in a taxi in

London, the taxi driver asked him where he was from. When he answered 'Britain', the taxi driver said 'Really?'. He said he felt insulted by the taxi driver's response. I thought: *This sounds bizarre. This man clearly doesn't look Caucasian, and he still has a Hong Kong accent. The taxi driver's curiosity was not unreasonable. Why was he upset?* It did not take me long to find the answer: **idolatry**.

A victim of bullying typically ends up wanting to become like the bully because subconsciously, he believes that if he could obtain the position of power and dominance that person had, he would be able to avoid being bullied again. If necessary, he could do the bullying. This is likewise for the dynamics between nations. Once subdued and dominated, a nation often aspires to become like the nation that did the subduing and dominating. That is why people from the nations that historically suffered Western imperialism and colonialism often aspire to become Westernised. They want to look like the Westerners, dress like the Westerners, have the lifestyle of the Westerners, and ultimately if they can, emigrate to a Western nation and take on the nationality of that nation.

Hence, what imperialism and colonialism tend to do is replace a nation's soul with another nation's soul, such that the people of the victim nation cannot be themselves – who God has created them to be specifically because the victim mentality propels them to strive to become someone else constantly.

This can be even more terrible than physical imperialism and colonialism. Physical imperialism and colonialism may be swept away by international opinions and retreat to history books, but 'cultural colonialism' nonetheless carries on until the soul of that nation can be healed. This is very subtle and usually hard to see because it is a way of being one grows up in, and people always surround him with the same way of being. To give

The Treasures of All Nations

a simple example: I have straight hair naturally, but for many years, I had my hair permed, believing that way was more beautiful. During the awakening of my national identity, one day, the Lord pointed out to me that this, too, is subconsciously trying to look more Western. Who would have known? Later, from speaking to a dear Ghanaian friend, I learnt that hair is a big part of black women's lives and a multi-billion dollar industry and that many black women desire straighter hair like that of the white women rather than their naturally curly hair. I thought, how fascinating! But then, I was only shocked to realise that this is nothing compared with what, sadly, many Chinese women are doing to themselves today through plastic surgeries, which have mainly become available and affordable in China: removing part of the jawbones to make the face narrower, planting a piece of material into the nose to make the bridge higher, slicing open the lateral canthi to make the eyes bigger... This is how far some are willing to go to become more Western!

The Treasures of All Nations

Oh Lord, help us!

The even greater concern is idolatry towards the West has also filtered into the church. From my experience with and observation of the believers in China, I noticed an interesting phenomenon: Western preachers are often held in higher regard than Chinese preachers. Chinese preachers that live in the West are often held in higher regard than the ones from the mainland. Teachings and prophecies that come from the West are usually taken at face value and considered authoritative.

There are indeed innumerable spiritual treasures in the Western church, which historically has a much deeper root in Christianity, and from which we can all benefit (as I have immensely, as mentioned at the start). Also, it is encouraging that technology and online means nowadays have made it possible for believers in China to access overseas Christian content. However, the problem is that erroneous teachings, unorthodox doctrines, and impure revelations from the West are also trying to seize the opportunity to come in, which I worry would lead the undiscerning astray. **For idolatry typically leads to BLIND submission, to a person or what a person says, without weighing** [3]. **This, in turn, causes widespread assimilation among the members of the body, good or bad** [4]. **I am thinking, if the churches in the nations that were once imperialised and colonised by Western powers all look up and conform to Western Christianity, would we not have uniformity at a universal level?** Besides, Western Christianity, though it has blessed many nations across the earth, in and of itself is not perfect. Having seen and experienced it myself over all these years, I am aware of its problems and challenges.

"What is the Church supposed to look like?" I asked the Lord.

The Treasures of All Nations

He first took me to Haggai 2:7-9: *"And I will shake all nations, so that* **THE TREASURES OF ALL NATIONS shall come in, and I will fill this house with glory**, *says the Lord of hosts.* **The SILVER is mine, and the GOLD is mine**, *declares the Lord of hosts. The latter glory of this house shall be greater than the former..."*. Whereas this scripture is often interpreted as worldly finance flowing into the Church, the Lord showed me that the 'silver' and 'gold' here represent believers of all nations who themselves are **the spiritual treasures** [5].

The Lord then led me to Isaiah 60, which lengthily describes the diverse types of 'treasures' coming in from different nations, including camels from Midian and Ephah, gold and frankincense from Sheba, flocks of Kedar, rams of Nebaioth, silver, and gold from Tarshish, and cypress, plane, and pine from Lebanon. These are associated with the sons and daughters coming from afar [6]. It dawned on me that the purpose for describing these different types of tributes from other nations is to convey that **diverse spiritual treasures or heritages from all nations are needed to make the house of the Lord beautiful and glorious** [7]. As it says in the same chapter, 'foreigners shall build up your walls' [8], and they shall 'beautify' the house of the Lord and make it 'glorious' [9]. Also, echoing Revelation 21:24-26 about the city of New Jerusalem, Isaiah 60:11 says: *"Your gates shall be open continually; day and night they shall not be shut, that people may bring to you **THE WEALTH OF THE NATIONS**, with **their kings** led in procession."* **Believers of different nations are the 'kings' – overcomers in Christ** [10], **and the Lord is the King of kings** [11]. **They shall bring themselves as the spiritual wealth of the nations to God's house.**

In my journey, the reconciliation with my Chinese national identity has brought me so much freedom and breakthrough. One of the areas is worship. For me, the instrument piano used to be associated with so many painful memories of my childhood; hours and hours of practising on my own while other children were playing outside, physical punishment for shirking or not playing correctly, and repeatedly being told that I was not good enough, a sense of failure that I had to live with for a big part of my adult life. For many years I felt nervous and deflated whenever I sat in front of a piano. Only at the beginning of 2020, encouraged by a dear brother, I started touching the keyboard again.

One day, I sat in front of my keyboard, wanting to attempt improvisation, but nothing came out. I got frustrated, so I gave up and started watching some videos of Messianic worship. While watching and listening, I was amazed by the confidence and joy those Jewish musicians displayed in using their Jewish sound to worship their Messiah, Yeshua. So, a thought came to mind: *What is the Chinese sound?* I got back to the keyboard and tried to play from my heart. I started with a few simple notes.

Then, suddenly, it was as if my fingers got loosened, and a whole beautiful song came out. I did not know how long it had passed, but when I finished, my face was covered with tears of gratitude. Redemption of creativity! New freedom! I realised that I could not do it before because, just as I was made to scrupulously stick to the notes written by famous Western composers when I was a child, I was trying to mimic the sound of Western worship. As soon as I let go of that, I was able to flow with the Spirit.

Today, I ever so enjoy worshipping the Father with my keyboard; it is my new love language to Him. Sometimes, when I cannot express something in words, sound does the job.

I have found that when we are comfortable in our own skin, not trying to be someone else, what we bring to God and the body tends to be the most anointed.

The Treasures of All Nations

There is a collection of over 1,800 Chinese worship songs called 'Canaan Hymns'. It was composed by Lü Xiaomin, a Chinese Christian peasant woman with hardly any education, under the inspiration of the Holy Spirit. Those songs may not have fancy arrangements like modern Western worship music and may even be considered a little '土' (uncouth), but they have brought millions to tears and are some of the most popular worship songs in Chinese churches. One of my personal favourites is called 'Lord, I praise You':

Oh Lord, we praise You, because You have chosen me
In this vast sea of people, You searched for me
Oh Lord, we praise You, because You have loved me
Your love fills the whole universe, the mountains, and the rivers
Your love has rescued many
Your love has inspired us to live on
Who will not bow down before You
Who will not sing aloud songs of praise to You

The Treasures of All Nations

Oh our great God, Oh our great Lord
It is You who have lifted us up from the dust
Words cannot express Your lovingkindness
Songs fail to extol Your righteousness
In this vast land, who will not give thanks and praise to You

'It is You who have lifted us up from the dust' – that is what the Lord has done for Lü Xiaomin, and for me. We are nothing but dust. Men trample on us, use us, and sacrifice us for their ambitions, but the Lord lifts us from the dust and makes us into clay... and then, vessels for honour! [12]

Distinguished individual believers have arisen from different continents and nations. However, to attain the eternal grandeur depicted in Haggai 2:7-9, Isaiah 60, and Revelation 21:24-26, the body is yet to hear and dance to the Chinese sound, the Indian sound, the African sound, the Latin American sound, etc., and is yet to taste the respective

The Treasures of All Nations

flavours of Christianity that we bring to the table in the household of God [13].

The Lord has manifested to me in different forms before; Indian, Middle Eastern, Caucasian (dark hair and blond hair, normal build and skinny build), and finally, a Chinese prince from the Qing dynasty with a shaven forehead and queue! He was dressed in white, with a beautiful Chinese bride standing next to Him. She had the type of quality described in 1 Peter 3:4. She wore an elaborate gold headdress and was richly arrayed in the traditional red Chinese wedding gown with gold embroidery. I know she represents those who make up the Bride in China. I am longing to see her one day become manifest, just as I am longing to see the Bride of Christ from all nations manifest with their distinct cultural characteristics.

We tend to flourish when we are free to be who God has created us to be in our cultures.

The Treasures of All Nations

From reading church history, I learnt that Henry Venn (1796-1873), the Anglican secretary to the Church Missionary Society from 1848 to 1879, was the first that encouraged missionaries to make the national church self-supporting, self-governing, and self-propagating with a national clergy, in direct opposition to the practice not only of converting the nationals to Christ but also civilising them in European ways under the paternal guidance of missionaries. John L. Nevius (1829-1893), a missionary to China and Korea, advocated the same principles. He also added the responsibility to train lay converts in the Bible and prayer, to serve as apprentices with missionaries, to be supported by the national churches instead of by missionaries, and to build churches in the architecture of the local area. '**The gospel + cultural freedom**' contributed to 10 years of great revivals in China and Korea from 1900 to 1910. [h]

A person that took it further was Hudson Taylor (1832-1905), who once famously said, "*If I had a thousand pounds, China should have it—if I had a thousand lives, China should have them. No! Not China, but Christ. Can we do too much for Him? Can we do enough for such a precious Saviour?*" [i] While other missionaries sought to preserve their British ways, Hudson Taylor was convinced that the Gospel would only take root on Chinese soil if missionaries were willing to affirm the culture of the people they were seeking to reach, following the apostle Paul's example in 1 Corinthians 9:20-22. He advocated 'identification with Chinese by wearing Chinese dress and queue' and 'indigenisation through training Chinese co-workers in self-governing, self-supporting and self-propagating principles' for the China Inland Mission. [j] The legacy of Hudson Taylor's works in China is immeasurable. We, as a nation, owe eternal gratitude to him.

Among the people whose nations used to be victims of imperialism and colonialism, an opposite response to idolatry can be sustained bitterness and resentment and seeking to establish identity in their cultural uniqueness, which leads to another type of idolatry. Sometimes, we can see idolatry and resentment present at the same time. For example, in China, on the one hand, many aspire to become more Western; on the other hand, they resent what Western nations did to our country and their 'hangover' from the past. So, seeking to find our place in the world, many try to take identity in the traditional Chinese culture and China's glorious ancient civilisation.

However, just like idolatry towards the West can influence the church, resentment towards bygone imperialism and current social elements associated with such can also influence the church, specifically confining the gospel to a social liberation message. Many Jews in Jesus' day thought He came to liberate them from the oppression of the Romans and set up a Messianic kingdom on earth, but God had something much more prominent in mind. He sent His Son to liberate all humanity from sin and the kingdom of darkness and set up an eternal kingdom that will supersede all other earthly kingdoms [14].

Poignant that it was with gunnery power that the doors to my nation were opened, which unfortunately created long-standing distrust of Christianity among the people, as it is seen to have come with Western imperialism. Nevertheless, at its worst, men's selfish greed was still able to be used by God to bring the light of the gospel of the kingdom to a land that was formerly in spiritual darkness. On account of the gospel mission of the West, millions and generations of Chinese have come to know Jesus, the Saviour of the world, God's truth and righteousness, and the love, joy, peace, and freedom that are only possible in Christ. Moreover, powerful testimonies have come out of China, inspiring many believers worldwide. All things work together for good. God always wins in the end!

The Treasures of All Nations

When the Lord first showed me the pain that Britain historically caused my nation, I jokingly said, "So, are You saying I have been serving the Philistines?" Joking aside, I HAVE FORGIVEN. I love Britain deeply, albeit not with idolatrous love anymore, but with God's love.

Sometimes, it feels as though my destiny is intertwined with this beloved nation. I have not told you that it was actually a British missionary and pioneering member of the China Inland Mission, William David Rudland (1839-1912), who planted the gospel in my hometown and set up the first main local church, which, after merging with a later Anglican church plant, pastored my late grandmother, who, in turn, prayed me into the kingdom. Great men and women of God in Britain then discipled me and poured so much into my life. Today, by God's grace, I am sowing back to the lives of believers in Britain – God truly works in mysterious ways! I believe the Lord has a glorious end-time mandate for the United Kingdom. I long to see it fulfilled; if God willing, I shall be part of it.

However, I will always be Chinese; that is who God created me to be. Whenever I am in China, I feel I am one part with the soil – from where the Lord took that lump of clay! I can feel everything in my surroundings and engage at every level. **Yet my identity is not in my 'Chineseness'. My identity is in the Lord.** While a nation typically sees its national identity and interests in this temporal world as the highest pursuit and seeks to take pride in and maximise such, from which comes nationalism, patriotism, and chauvinism... the truth is the destiny of a nation assigned by God is so much greater and higher. Jesus said, *"You know that the rulers of the Gentiles lord it over them, and their great ones exercise authority over them. It shall not be so among you. But whoever would be great among you must be your servant, and whoever would be first among you must be your slave.* [15]*"* Nations that are the greatest in God's eyes and most esteemed in heaven are not the ones with the most significant military and economic might but the ones that serve other nations most. Like those sheep nations in Matthew 25:31-46 (KJV) that satisfied the hungry and thirsty, welcomed in strangers, clothed the naked, and visited the sick and imprisoned, they will inherit the kingdom of heaven. **And this is an eternal heritage and a testimony that will be remembered forever.**

A vast amount of injustice has indeed been done to many nations, and the peoples of those nations still suffer the spiritual aftermath of such. However, we have the power to choose whether to take the matter of justice into our own hands or commit it to the Great Judge. And for all of us, whichever nations we are from, we are free to choose whether to set our eyes on our interests in this temporal world or on the Kingdom of our Lord and His Christ that will never be destroyed.

The Treasures of All Nations

I grew up in a small city surrounded by lofty mountains in Eastern China. When I was a child, I was often mesmerised by the sunset in the west, the soft orange glow behind the shadowy mountains echoed by the fiery red clouds above. Time and time again, I revelled in the tranquillity of such a sight and the mystery of what lies beyond in the west, as if I could rise on the wings of the dusk and fly all the way there to find out. The conclusion of a day promises a new dawn with infinite possibilities.

Twenty-odd years later, here I am in the west, looking through a glass window of a fast-moving train. Again, there is the sunset! Red and orange, beautiful as always, yet somewhat has lost its charm.

Ah, knowledge is a killer of fascination!

I have tasted, seen, and been acquainted with all that the west has to offer and have found that it is also crying for hope and redemption. Standing where many children of the east today, like the then child me, are still aspiring to be, I sighed a deep sigh... If only they knew it was just a mirage. After all, the sun sets on the west, and our pilgrimages towards it will eventually lead us back to the east; it goes around and is nothing but a striving after wind.

But contentment is found in those who are reconciled with God and grow to be the sons that He has created them to be, and fulfilment in those who are reconciled with their fathers and mothers and, ultimately, with themselves, as the individuals and peoples embellished with unique qualities and multi-coloured heritages, in our God-given identity.

Neither the east nor the west is our home, but the eternal city above that has foundations, into which the kings of the earth shall bring the glory and the honour of the nations [16].

The Treasures of All Nations

(to be continued...)

1. (Isa 64:8) **2.** (Isa 54:11; Mat 11:28) **3.** (1Th 5:21; 1Co 14:29) **4.** (Psa 115:4-8; 135:15-18; Mat 15:14; 1Co 12:17-19) **5.** (Mal 3:3; Zec 13:9; 1Pe 1:7) **6.** (Isa 60:4,9) **7.** (1Pe 2:4-7; Eph 2:20-22; 1Co 3:9) **8.** (Isa 60:10) **9.** (Isa 60:7,9,13) **10.** (Rev 3:21) **11.** (Rev 17:14; 19:16) **12.** (2Ti 2:21, NKJV) **13.** (Eph 2:19) **14.** (Dan 2:44; 7:13-14; Rev 11:15; Heb 12:27-28) **15.** (Mat 20:25-27) **16.** (Eph 2:19; Php 3:20; Heb 11:10,13-16; Rev 21)

a. Henry Kissinger. (2011). On China. Publisher: Penguin Press. ISBN 9781594202711.
b. Peter Ward Fay. (1998). Opium War, 1840-1842. Publisher: University North Carolina. ISBN: 9780807847145.
c. Opium trade – History & Facts. Encyclopedia Britannica. Retrieved 3 July 2018.
d. Daily News. London. 5 January 1863. Retrieved via British Newspaper Archive.
e. Hsin-Pao Chang. (1965). Commissioner Lin and the Opium War. Publisher: Harvard University Press. ISBN: 9780674145511.
f. Steve Tsang. (2007). A modern history of Hong Kong. Publisher: I.B. Tauris. ISBN: 9781845114190.
g. Ha-Joon Chang. (2010). Bad Samaritans: The Myth of Free Trade and the Secret History of Capitalism. Publisher: Bloomsbury Press. ISBN: 9781596915985.
h. Earle E. Cairns. (1996). Christianity Through the Centuries: A History of the Christian Church. Publisher: Zondervan. ISBN 9780310208129
i. A.J. Broomhall. (1983). Hudson Taylor and China's Open Century: If I had a Thousand Lives. Publisher: Hodder and Stoughton Religious. ISBN 978-0340323922.
j. Daniel W. Bacon. (1984). From Faith To Faith. Publisher: O M F Books. ISBN 978-9971972035.

Printed in Great Britain
by Amazon